COOK LIKE A TIE-DOWN ROPER

Menus and Memories

Jody Westbrook Bergman

Photography by David Burke
davidburkephotography.net

AuthorHouse™
1663 Liberty Drive
Bloomington, IN 47403
www.authorhouse.com
Phone: 833-262-8899

Because of the dynamic nature of the Internet, any web addresses or links contained in this book may have changed since publication and may no longer be valid. The views expressed in this work are solely those of the author and do not necessarily reflect the views of the publisher, and the publisher hereby disclaims any responsibility for them.

Any people depicted in stock imagery provided by Getty Images are models, and such images are being used for illustrative purposes only. Certain stock imagery © Getty Images.

This book is printed on acid-free paper.

ISBN: 978-1-6655-1715-7 (sc)
978-1-6655-1717-1 (hc)
978-1-6655-1716-4 (e)

Library of Congress Control Number: 2021903342

Print information available on the last page.

Published by AuthorHouse 03/02/2021

Dedication

To my family and my friends,

When I've dined with you, we enjoyed a meal and I learned something from you that enriched my knowledge.

When I cooked for you, I intended to enrich your life and I learned something from you that enriched my life.

When you cooked for me, I was blessed and honored and I re-learned that the gift of friendship and service is life-affirming.

When I've cooked with you, I learned new kitchen tricks, new recipes and new stories, but even better, I've learned new things about you and we created a memory!

Thank you for being a part of my Kitchen Journey!

Jody Westbrook Bergman is a learner, an author, and a collector of menus. She loves to cook and open the house to welcome visitors from near and far. Gathering menus and stories has been her way of remembering her life for the last fifty years. Jody's been a teacher, a principal, central office administrator, college professor, and Executive Director of Learning Forward-TX.

She is the author of Creating the Capacity for Change and has taught courses in leadership development and constructive change in education across the US and in Canada. She lives in Roanoke, Texas with her husband, Mike and their horse, Roanie. She and Mike are very active in their church.

Jody has been a member of a learning community called the Star Learners for 25 years. Taking turns designing and facilitating each other's learning, the group has been an integral part of Jody's continuing interest in learning about anything and everything.

Jody and Mike love to "waltz across Texas," literally and figuratively, going to old Dance Halls to enjoy some boot scootin' and C & W music. On their journeys, they stop to visit old friends and new steak places.

Her watch never has to tell her to STAND. She practices yoga twice a week, hits the gym for cardio and strength training twice a week and counts dancing with Mike as both exercise and fun.

As one reader said, "Reading these stories makes me want to invite myself to your house, eat a pimento cheese sandwichand hear more stories."

To contact the author: drjodybergman@gmail.com

Table of Contents

Introduction

The Cook Meets the Cowboy

Natalie Depree . . . taught me that cooking and storytelling make the most delightful co-conspirators. Either was good alone, but in communion with each other they could rise to the level of ecstasy.

Pat Conroy

I was not born on a ranch; a ranch was born in me. My report from the fourth grade describes how I would raise cows and horses.

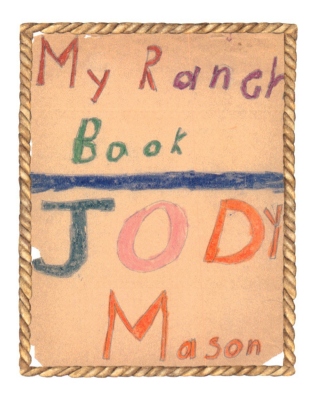

My friends across the United States and Canada refer to me as *Texas Jody.* Having attended an annual international conference of educators for thirty years, I would often hear people say, "I saw your hat and knew that Texas Jody had arrived!"

For all of my adult life, family and friends have given me western décor, pillows, clothing and rodeo memorabilia. I wear a black felt Cowboy hat in the fall and winter months, a straw in the spring and summer months. I have three pairs of identical black Ferrini western boots. The oldest pair is for arenas, where dust and dirt are the main surroundings. The middle pair is for dancing as they are broken in just right! The newest pair is for Date Night, formal events, and church services. I have turquoise boots, two-tone gold and brown boots, beige ropers and brown short boots with turquoise stitching and turquoise rhinestones on the toes.

You may wonder how I created the relationship of cooking to tie-down roping and rodeo life. My husband, Mike, introduced me to rodeos and tie-down roping. I asked him to describe all the steps to be successful in tying down a calf. As Mike outlined the steps to a successful tie-down, I, of course, started taking notes. Family and friends know me as The Notetaker. I have many years of notes taken during sermons at a variety of churches. Should you ever need a sermon topic and outline, contact me.

As Mike talked, I wasn't enchanted with the steps, but I was (and am) enchanted by Mike, so I was paying close attention.

Mike's name first appeared as a guest on a menu in March of 2011. It was an unusual group—no one knew each other, but they all knew me. When he said he was coming to town to see his cousin, I offered that I was having a few people over for dinner, and that he should join us. He did not hesitate. I did not realize it until months later, but Mike would become the love of my life.

Mike is an enigma in the most wonderful ways. He is well-educated and professionally successful, but he doesn't need anyone to know that. He donates blood every eight weeks to help other people get healthy. He delivers food from our church to schools so kids can take food home for the weekend. He gives away food from his impressive garden, which I have labeled The Garden of Fecundity. He would tell you none of that. Many people he meets think he's just a regular Good Ol' Boy. He is truly a rough and tumble cowboy but can step into a tuxedo and dazzle the eyes. When he wears his army dress blue uniform to a Military Ball, reflecting his officer status as a helicopter pilot in Vietnam, you can see people admiring and respecting him. Put him in jeans and a stiffly starched western shirt, a black felt hat, and one of his many pairs of boots, turn on classic Country Western music, and he can dance your heart right out of your chest and put it squarely in his hands. His hands hold mine during worship services at our church. His hands create structures and repair anything that needs attention. His magical hands are capable, loving, gentle, productive hands. His hands iron my clothes! So, when he talks about roping, I'm listening.

Actually, when he talks about anything, I'm listening. Unless it's a replay of the Aztec Bowl in 1966, in which he played for Tarleton State University. Then, I pretend to listen, because at this point, I could tell that story. It's a great story.

As I looked at the list of steps Mike had given, it occurred to me that it was similar to my planning lists for menus and cooking, some actions obvious and some so subtle no one else would know I was doing them. I then started listening to rodeo phrases and found that so many of them could reflect cooking behaviors and terms. And that, my ranch hand friends, is how this book was born!

This memoir is about the importance of enjoying cooking, eating, and making memories with people you love. It is about funny and not-so-funny memories evoked from reading the menus I've kept since 1972. It includes favorite recipes and tips learned over the last fifty years, but more importantly, the gift of learning and fun times created by cooking with friends and family.

My kitchen is the original footprint of our house, which was built in 1954. My kitchen is one of my happy places in our home. A charming and warm family, the Prislicka family, claimed this as their home for many years, and their personalities and fun-filled memories must have been absorbed into the DNA of the house. We've been dancing at the local Czech Hall with them. They can handle a polka and a beer. At the same time.

First time visitors almost always comment on how welcoming the home feels. The kitchen has been updated in terms of looks and better appliances. Compared to the size of kitchens in newer homes, it is small, but as our neighbor Natalie says, it is an amazing and mighty kitchen! The cabinets are a sea-blue, with black iron hardware and appliances. Some of the cabinets have glass fronts, which is a nice incentive to not overstuff a cabinet. The countertop is marble and looks well-loved, which is a euphemism for etched and scratched, but at least it is not stained.

The sink has one huge bowl, very deep and made of granite. It is so large that I think you could bathe two babies at one time. That's a terrible idea—two at one time! Over the sink is a huge window, which looks out over thirty oak trees, our horse pen, and an arena where Roanie, our horse, grazes, rolls in the dirt, and chomps on apples. I can also see the neighbors' horse pen, where two ponies, Tater Tot and Mama, live.

We have wonderful neighbors. Brandon is as level as the top of a table, can fix and build anything, and he and Mike make a lot of noise with stereo leaf blowers, chain saws, wood-chippers, and other loud machinery. Natalie is a go-getter, very creative and very artistic. They are attentive parents of two cute kids that Mike and I call our "bonus grands." Mason, age six, sees Mike outside and yells. "Mike! I'm outside!"

Mike yells back, "Come on over and swing!" Maddie is only a year old, and we anticipate it will not be long before she runs over with Mason.

Tater Tot and Mama like to kick their food bucket to get attention. The day they arrived, Roanie started running around his pen, and the ponies started running around their pen. It was a very exciting and communal greeting and bonding. I love to watch them when a yellow feral cat runs through the two pens. All of the horses stop and stare at the cat, almost as if they are afraid of that tiny cat! Sometimes, in the midst of sautéing onions for a soup or chopping veggies to slide into the air roaster, I wash my hands and stop working for a moment to appreciate the beauty and the serenity of the view.

One of the aromas most often drifting through the air is fudge cake, which is richer than brownies, and is always a hit when I take it to someone's house. Or perhaps the combination of vanilla and almond will greet you when I bake my Pound Cake, which is sometimes divided among four families. You'll note that there are some differences in the recipe shown in the picture from 1942 and the printed recipe given here. Things have changed through the years!

Pound cake (with Buttermilk)

1 cp. shortening
3 cps sugar
6 eggs (separated)
3 cps flour
1 cp. buttermilk
½ teaspoon salt
¼ teaspoon soda
2 teasp. lemon or orange extract

Cream shortening & sugar - add eggs
one at a time - (add flavoring - add flour,
salt, & soda, sifted together) alternately
with buttermilk. be beating and end with

Pound Cake with Buttermilk

Preheat your oven to 350°. Generously spray a tube pan (not a Bundt pan) with nonstick baking spray.

1/2 cup (1 stick) butter at room temperature

1/2 cup shortening, cut into small pieces

3 cups sugar

6 eggs at room temperature

3 cups flour

1/2 teaspoon baking soda

1/2 teaspoon salt

1 cup buttermilk

1 tablespoon cornstarch

1 teaspoon vanilla extract

1 teaspoon almond extract

1. Using a stand mixer, blend the butter, shortening, sugar and eggs.
2. Whisk together the flour, baking soda and salt.
3. Add the flour mixture, about 1/3 cup at a time, to the wet butter mixture, alternating with a few ounces of the buttermilk until all is well-blended.
4. Stop and scrape the sides 2-4 times so that you catch all the ingredients and ensure proper mixing.
5. Beat in the cornstarch.
6. Beat in the extracts (options are listed in the **TIPS & HINTS** section)

Bake for 55-65 minutes. Test by inserting a cake tester tool, toothpick, or skewer into the cake until it comes out clean (meaning there is no sticky batter when you remove the tester).

Cool for 10 minutes in the pan, then turn it out onto a cake plate. Let it cool another 30 minutes before cutting.

Hide it until you're ready to serve it, otherwise your family will smell it and start eating it immediately!

The kitchen is open to several gathering spaces. It feeds into a room we call the jukebox room, because it holds a 1958 Seeburg jukebox. For a quarter, you can play two songs, unless the jukebox decides to just play one for you. We provide quarters so that there is always music. There's also a baby grand piano in that room, which leads two steps down into the fireplace room, with overstuffed leather chairs, bookshelves, lots of books and family photos. The kitchen also feeds into our main living space. With all that open space, we can have large groups here. Or we can host a small dance . . . which we have! One summer, the air-conditioning was not working in our Sunday School classroom, so Mike and I made a huge pot of coffee, some blueberry coffee cake iced with cream cheese, set out lots of chairs and opened the doors to greet our class and proceeded with our lesson. I like that juxtaposition—Sunday School in the morning, a Rock and Roll dance in the evening!

In this book, some names have been changed to protect the innocent and the guilty, especially the couple that came for a 7 PM dinner and stayed until 2 AM.

This book is not about roping, rodeos, or being a cowboy. It's not solely about recipes, but many are included, and every effort has been made to give proper attribution. It is not about perfect recipes nor is it about perfect menus. It is a memoir which happens to include menus and recipes.

I've been asked why I started keeping menus. I'm guessing I was an insecure cook. Well, all of me is insecure, and journaling is a way to keep neediness organized. Someone was coming to dinner and my randomness knew to deploy some sequential, linear strategies. So, I wrote out a menu. Not too long after that, someone else was coming to dinner, so I wrote that menu, too. After that, it was much like, "Run, Forrest, run!" I just kept writing my menus for dinner guests, but also included meals I've taken to friends who were ill, experienced the loss of a beloved family member, or those who just needed a surprise!

Fast-forward to 2015 and my participation in a *Cook & Write* retreat, hosted and facilitated by two long-time and very talented friends, Beverly Charles and Lyn Mefford. As a part of the retreat, Beverly and Lyn encouraged us to bring artifacts of our cooking history for display on a community table. Participants brought their grandmother's cast iron skillet or other sweet family memorabilia. Some brought cookbooks. Some even brought tour itineraries. I guess that made them think of food they liked while on vacation. I enjoyed viewing their itineraries and hearing about the food they enjoyed while traveling. And many of the participants brought family recipes. The artifact that I took was two binders with labels that said, *Menus 1973—2012* and *Menus 2013—2019*. I had menus that were older than some of our participants!

As other participants talked about their artifacts and the memories evoked, I had an *aha* moment. I had my memories of almost fifty years of cooking for others already recorded. During the writing portion of the retreat, we were challenged to write about our artifact. It occurred to me how complex but also how much fun it is to put a meal together. During the feedback portion of our writing time, I verbally compared it to what my cowboy husband had taught me about the complexity of tying down a calf that needs to be transported to a vet. You don't just walk up and throw a halter on them. It's the same premise in preparing a meal. You don't just walk in the kitchen and set things out at the last minute; there are many steps in planning and creating a great meal. The writing group laughed and asked for more stories. I was encouraged by the group to develop the stories and share them. I thought it would be fun to share, not just my memories, but what I've learned along the way.

My menus are written on all sorts of paper. Many are written on notebook paper just because that fits nicely in a three-ring binder. Some are on formal note cards. Do people even use formal stationery anymore? Do people even write notes anymore other than email? Text? Instagram? Some menus are on conference notepads; some are on flowery notepaper. In recent years, menus are often recorded on my computer, with my preferred font and size. I tend to repeat successful menus. Hand-written menus are still my go-to, because I can record the small steps and timeline on the back. I often, but not always, record the cookbook and page number of a recipe on the back of the menu. It may be from my personal collection of recipes, which includes those that I've been given or torn out of magazines, newspapers, or other publications as well as those I've printed from on-line resources. These are kept in my three notebooks with dividers and sections that make sense to me. That way, if I want to re-create a menu for a new group, I have my references ready.

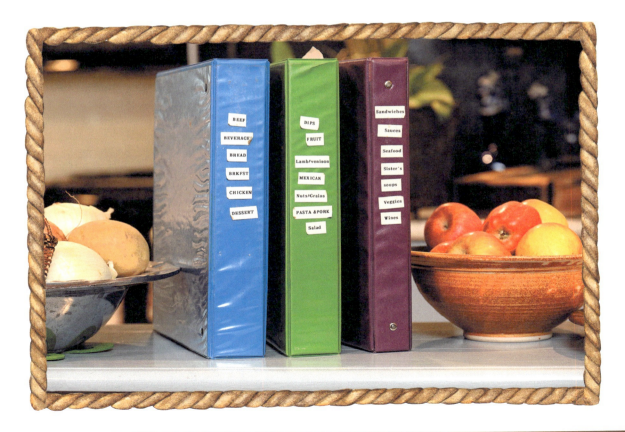

Let me introduce you to my aunt, Dorothy Foote Elmore, who was the source of some of my favorite memories and recipes. She was always addressed as *Sister* or *Sister Dorothy* and was my early inspiration for cooking. She was the manager of a middle school cafeteria. She went to work, came home, fixed dinner, watched TV, and went to bed early, as school cafeteria workers have to arrive at school before daylight to get lunches started.

On Sundays, Sister and her family met us at Pleasant Grove First Baptist Church, where she, my mother, and grandmother attended from 1927 until it was disbanded in the early nineties. Sister dabbled with gardening, had great sewing skills, and made the sweetest tea, with just the right amount of sugar and lemon. She had lots of interests and talents, but to my knowledge, she really had no hobbies.

Sister often adapted dishes from school cafeteria recipes for us, my favorite being her Snickerdoodle cookies. Even today, if I detect the aroma of cinnamon, I immediately visualize soft, buttery, Snickerdoodles with ample cinnamon and sugar on top, ready to melt in my mouth. I wish she could make me some cookies right now and serve them with sweet tea!

Here's a little bit of history about Snickerdoodles. The cookie first appeared in American cookbooks in the late 1800s. It's said to have been the favorite cookie of James Buchanan, Jr., the 15th President of the United States.

There are as many variations for Snickerdoodle recipes as there are pieces of hay in a round bale. Everyone has their favorite, and some claim that theirs is the *best ever* Snickerdoodle. I'll just claim that the one I offer here is *above average*. My recipe is a hybrid of the many, many recipes I've tried. I've added ingredients, removed ingredients, tried the advice of several cooks and decided some of those ideas worked and some did not. No one has ever turned down one of my Snickerdoodles and to my knowledge, no one has ever thrown one away.

Snickerdoodle Cookies

Preheat the oven to 350°.

Dry mixture

2-3/4 cups all-purpose flour

2 teaspoons cream of tartar

1 teaspoon baking soda

Scant 1/2 teaspoon ground cinnamon (careful—too much will make your cookie a little on the bitter side)

Just under 1/2 teaspoon salt

Wet mixture

1 cup sugar

1/2 cup packed brown sugar

1 cup butter, about half-way melted

1/4 cup shortening, cut into small pieces

2 eggs at room temperature

2 teaspoons vanilla extract

Cinnamon sugar mixture

1/4 cup sugar

2 teaspoons ground cinnamon

Directions

1. <u>Dry Ingredients</u>: Whisk together the flour, cream of tartar, baking soda, ground cinnamon, and salt. Do this in a large bowl as you will be adding the wet ingredients.

2. <u>Wet ingredients</u>: In a separate bowl, mix the sugar, brown sugar, butter, shortening, eggs and the vanilla. Whisk until it's smooth.

3. Add the wet ingredients to the dry ingredients, stirring just until well combined. Cover and refrigerate for 45 minutes.

4. Remove the dough from the refrigerator. Make balls about the size of a walnut, only more cylindrical. I make mine about 3/4 the length of my thumb, which is about 1 1/2 inches. I measure the first one carefully, then I just "eye-ball" the rest.

5. Roll the balls in the cinnamon sugar mixture and place about 2 inches apart on a parchment lined baking sheet. I tried a cooking mat, parchment paper, a greased cookie Sheet (Don't do that! Your cookies will slide off the cookie sheet), and an insulated cookie sheet. They all turn out about the same; the parchment paper is the easiest clean-up.

6. Bake 8-9 minutes.

7. Let cool on the cookie sheet for 4-5 minutes, then move to a cooling rack.

8. Eat one for Quality Assurance and prepare for an onslaught of family and friends who want one!

When Sister retired, some of her family members asked her what in the world was she going to do. Remember, she had no hobbies. When asked that question, she replied, "I am going to learn to paint. I want to use oils and watercolor. I want to paint bluebonnets, cardinals in the snow, and old houses." I'm not sure if we looked shocked, delighted, or skeptical, but I am pretty sure we all nodded and offered polite responses such as, "Wow. I didn't know you had an interest in painting. That's wonderful." Perhaps we doubted her ability and interest, and if so, we were certainly wrong.

And paint she did! Sister painted beautiful paintings, giving them away to nieces, nephews, and friends, but she also sold lots of paintings for lots of money. I was inspired to see her reinvent herself, finding joy in the process of painting, in the generosity of sharing, and in earning some money as well. She was still painting well into her eighties and had a stroke while painting. Having an ultimately fatal stroke while you're doing something you love seems to be a somewhat comforting departure.

In the early 1950s, Sister began making a recipe for Fruit Salad that makes about 24 cups. It feeds a small posse and is unusual in that it's a multi-day process, but worth it! It takes a day to drain the cans of fruit, the sauce is a cooked sauce which then has to cool before it is added to fresh whipped cream. The photo of several iterations of the recipe is a testament to the need to STOP sharing recipes over the phone and scrawling them on any piece of paper you can find! Luckily, it is offered here after testing it one more time!

Fruit Salad

<u>The fruit</u>

2 (6 ounce) jars maraschino cherries

2 (18-20 ounce) cans pineapple tidbits, saving 1 cup of this juice

2 (14-15 ounce) cans apricots

3 (14-15 ounce) cans pears

3 (14-15 ounce) cans peaches

2 bananas, cut into small slices

1. Drain the cherries before draining the other fruits. You don't want that pretty red juice all over the other fruit.
2. Add in the apricots, pears, peaches, and pineapple tidbits in a very large colander (ours is 16 inches in diameter). This process takes several hours to completely drain all the juice off. To hasten the process, I often walk by and mash the fruits with the back of a large spoon.
3. When it's time to serve, move the fruits to a pretty glass bowl, and add the bananas. The bananas need to be the very last thing to add before folding in the sauce. You don't want them to turn brown.
4. Fold in the sauce.

<u>The sauce</u>

1 cup pineapple juice (saved from when all fruits are drained)

4 Tablespoons lemon juice

3 Tablespoons flour

2/3 cup sugar

A light *sprinkle* of salt

1. Cook this until it becomes thick.
2. In a separate bowl, beat 2 eggs.
3. Get a large spoonful of the cooked mix and stir/whisk it *vigorously* into the eggs, not allowing the mixture to harden the eggs. When fully incorporated, add the egg mixture into the cooked sauce, whisk a little more and remove it from the heat. Let it cool completely.
4. Whip 1/2 cup heavy whipping cream until slightly peaking and fold the cooled sauce with the whipped cream.

Chill and prepare for happy diners.

Danielle Kartes, in *Meant to Share,* offers what I consider a beautiful philosophy:

We are meant for community, and our hearts long for fellowship and laughter. We are designed for joy, specifically the kind that arises from time well spent with others. Sometimes we want to wait until things feel perfect. We will have people over when we know them better, or we will give when we have more to spare. I know that God loves openhandedness.

TIPS & HINTS

- When you make the Snickerdoodle balls, *lightly* spray your hands with non-stick spray to keep the dough from caking on your hands. The key word is *lightly*; too much will add oil to the cookies.

- Don't let cookies or cakes cool longer than the recommended amount of time. They will get too hard and will not release from the pan or cookie sheet and will crumble. You shouldn't crumble as well if this happens. Most people will laugh **with** you and start eating the crumbled cake or cookies.

- When making the sauce for the fruit salad recipe, don't add the egg to the hot mixture as it will become a scrambled egg in your sauce. Instead, take a bit of the hot mix and add it to the egg and stir like crazy until it is incorporated. Then, add it to the sauce and stir or whisk until it is blended.

- I like to have a system for finding recipes I've used and want to make again. For example, I have a recipe for Mexican Corn Relish that can be served as a salad, a dip or a garnish on a Taco Salad. I keep it in my notebook in the section labeled *Mexican Food,* but it could go in the *Salad* or *Appetizer* sections. When I list it on a menu, I circle the word *Mexican* which reminds me where in my notebooks or computer files I'll find the recipe.

- I sometimes change the extract flavor for the Pound Cake. My favorite is to use both almond and vanilla, but I often use orange extract or Amaretto liqueur. I've read that coconut and rum extracts are also nice.

Now it's time to employ the tie-down roper's techniques!

- Mount your horse (create your menu),

- Nod your head and let the lineman know to let the calf out (make your list of groceries, your timeline, and what you need for your table setting),

- Step off, which is *not* the same as jumping off (do as much as you can prior to guests arriving, set your table and prepare your meal),

- Focus, focus, focus and visualize how much fun it will be to feed your family and friends!

Chapter One

Nineteen Steps to a Tie-down: Planning and Preparing a Meal

No matter what happens, never apologize for your cooking.

Julia Childs

There are events and moments in life that are an all or nothing. You can't be kinda pregnant. You either are, or you aren't! You can't be kinda four years old or kinda seventy years old. You are, or you aren't!

A tie-down roper cannot kinda tie down a calf. He either does it or does not do it successfully.

To be a successful tie down roper, you must:

- Mount your horse,
- have the piggin' string between your teeth,
- your rope in your hand,
- sit forward in the saddle,
- nod your head to the gatekeeper, signaling that it's time to open the gate and release the calf,
- leave the box, but not too fast, because if you leave too soon, and break the barrier, it will cost you a ten second penalty,
- swing your rope two-three times,
- fling your rope,
- and if you rope the calf—YAY! YIPPEE!
- BUT! You are not finished! Then you must:

- Step off of your horse,
- do not let your foot or boot or spurs or anything else, for that matter, get caught in the rope or stirrup,
- *run* down the rope, which means run down the length of the rope, sliding your hands along the rope,
- flank the calf: That means that you pick up the calf and lay it ever so gently on the ground,
- remove the piggin' string from your teeth,

- tie three feet together,
- throw your arms in the air (this shows the flagman that you're done),
- run back to your horse,
- allow slack in the rope,
- pray the calf stays down for six seconds.

If all of the above goes well, the Flagman throws a flag up in the air and a bunch of cowboys run. They do NOT walk; they run to untie the calf and release it from roper bondage. That is only nineteen steps to a successful event that is over anywhere between eight and eighteen seconds. Not minutes . . . seconds.

And then, you are finished!

That's pretty much what it's like in planning, preparing and serving a meal—it requires specific steps, including pre-planning what you are serving for the meal:

Pre-planning: Create your menu

- Appetizers
- Entrée
- Sides
- Bread
- Dessert
- Beverages

Planning steps: Make your list of groceries, your timeline, and what you need for your table setting.

Serving steps: Do as much prior to guests arriving as you possibly can, such as setting the table, have items ready to pop in the oven, Instant Pot, Air Roaster, or on the grill.

Serving: Visualize how much fun it will be to feed family and friends.

Read on for tips about creating **menus**, **logistics**, your own **recipes**, options for **table settings** and **serving**.

Menu: How do you create excellent menus?

You do not have to make up new menus every time you make a meal! Start with recording menus in a notebook or on your computer. Don't let them wander around the wilderness of your computer. Am I the only one who procrastinates about creating folders? Create a folder for menus or write them out and put them in a chronological notebook.

Take notes when you are at other people's homes, take pictures at restaurants of meals that look appetizing, then recreate it, paring down the menu or the number of sides.

Check out menus offered on-line or by the pros of cooking. I really enjoy and frequently use Martha Stewart's *Dinner at Home: 52 Quick Meals to Cook for Family and Friends* as well as her other quick cookbooks. These offer complete menus and I rarely, but sometimes, use an entire menu. If the menu lists some sort of green salad and I already have a favorite I want to use, I substitute mine.

Ina Garten also offers books with complete menus. Again, I use them as a guideline and substitute seasonal items. True confession here, I usually have a new recipe that I want to try and will prepare that instead of following suggested menus. Make no mistake, you will *not* go wrong following menus described by either of these two cooks. Their recipes are vetted and tested to perfection.

Compare the preciseness of the professional cook's menus to those found in church, school or club cookbooks. I absolutely adore and treasure those kinds of cookbooks because it's real people sharing their family favorites. But just know that they probably have not been tested before being published and you might have an occasional surprise or mishap. The reading is as good as the recipes. I love the descriptors I've read. *This one will bring the men-folk running from the fields,* or *cook until it's not shiny on top.* Then there was this adorable descriptor, *Aunt Ella says layer this salad with the eggs at the bottom, but Aunt Clara says the eggs go on the top!*

One of my kitchen buddies with whom I cook frequently (you'll meet my kitchen buddies in Chapter Four) offers this stress-reducer. If you have a complicated entrée, serve very simple sides, such as steamed or roasted veggies or baked potatoes. If you have a simple entrée, such as Roast Chicken or Grilled Burgers, offer a more complicated side and a simple dessert such as sherbet layered with fruit and a delicate cookie from your local bakery. You already know that a Snickerdoodle Cookie is a quick and timeless treat!

Are there overlaps of ingredients—for example, do you have a cheese-based appetizer AND a cheese-based side? Change one of them! That's too much cheese!

Logistics: Avoiding an organizational mess!

- The timing of cooking different dishes—you don't want three items that require your oven at the same time, even if they use the same temperature. Multiple items alter the timing of each item. If you have two ovens—great!
- Will it be a buffet, plated and served to each person, or homestyle where you take platters and bowls to the serving table?
- Can anything be made ahead? Ina Garten, The Barefoot Contessa, acclaimed chef and author of nine cookbooks, says in *Make It Ahead,*

What's important about learning to cook ahead is to know what you can make in advance and what you need to do at the last minute.

Create Your Own Recipes:

Keep trying new recipes and create your own. When I want to improve something that is popular (for example, a pork roast or a meatloaf), and every chef has a recipe for it, I look at recipes online, in favorite cookbooks, or in my notebooks. I research the latest recipes and note similarities and differences. I check out options for my InstantPot, Ninja Air Fryer/Roaster/And Everything Else, and my 3-in-1 Multifunction crockpot. I follow the similarities and select the differences that I think we will prefer.

For example, meatloaf similarities are a combination of meat: beef, pork and/or veal, a binder of crackers, bread or breadcrumbs, an egg or two, and onions and bell peppers. I developed our favorite recipe by what we like. I use Italian breadcrumbs because I like the seasoning and parsley mixture, but I add a little more moisture by adding just a splash of half and half cream, heavy cream, or evaporated milk. One recipe offered that onions should be sautéed before adding to the meat mixture, otherwise they are too crunchy. I agree with that, so I sauté mine, but really, it is a personal preference. I never put green bell peppers in my meatloaf.

Usually, it works out when I create my own recipe by combining favorites, but not always. I recently made a chocolate cream pie from a newspaper recipe. As I read it and compared it to two of my favorite chefs' recipes, I noticed the newspaper version had lots more liquid than the other two, but I did not adjust the amount of liquid. I should have adjusted it. The pie was so rich with chocolate and lusciously piled high with a whipped cream mixture that included Mascarpone cheese, which added depth. Of course, it was made for a guest, who laughed with me when I said, "Oops. We'll be serving this in a bowl and not on a dessert plate!" I renamed it Rich Chocolate Soup!

Table Setting/Serving:

Your first big decision is if you want to serve your meal **buffet** style, **seated and plated** or **homestyle/family style**. I almost always prefer buffet for a couple of reasons. First, people can select what they prefer and secondly, unless you have a helper in the kitchen, you are running out two plates at a time and your guests are waiting for you to be seated. We don't use homestyle/family style at our house because our dining table is around the corner and down some steps. It's still a comfy and warm option. It just doesn't work at our house.

If you decide to go buffet, another decision needs to be made: will you put the dishes on the table or as a part of the buffet line? I like to put them on the tables because it makes the table look complete and inviting, and people can choose where, and with whom, they want to sit. They select a plate and head to the buffet line.

What dishes will you use? I have lots of options and depending on the formality of the dinner or what I'm serving, I choose accordingly.

For example, I have some heavy pottery with swirls of dark blue and turquoise, juxtaposed with terra cotta earthy tones. I love this dinnerware for Mexican Chef Salad or other salad entrees. The background colors contrast well with the colors of the lettuces and veggies.

In my early days of serving Mexican Chef Salad, I mixed it all up, even dressing it with what the recipe said. Now I chop all the ingredients the night before, store them in the refrigerator in the dish in which I will serve them, and let guests build their own salad. I usually offer at least two protein choices and two or three dressings.

Choices that I include for a Taco Salad Bar include (and I offer them in this order):

- soft tortillas, both corn and flour
- tortilla chips
- two kinds of lettuce, usually iceberg and romaine
- baby spinach
- three kinds of onions, chopped: green, purple and sweet yellow
- tomatoes
- two kinds of grated cheeses: Monterey Jack and Cheddar
- jalapeno slices: pickled and fresh
- three kinds of beans: pinto, black, kidney
- sliced peppers: red and yellow
- salsa: mild and medium
- toasted pepitas

You'll notice in the pictures that I have wooden trays made of recycled barnwood that slide over my sink to hide last minute dishes and utensils which hold the bowls with options for guests to build their salad. You'll see one picture of the night before with post it notes reminding me where to place bowls. The other picture is how it looks when I put out all the bowls.

When I serve sea scallops with Spinach Layered Salad, I will use one of my sets of white dishes because the white background shows off the food but doesn't overwhelm it. Yes, I have more than one set of white dishes, but mostly I have a variety of white dinner plates and white lunch/dessert/salad plates rather than complete sets. I buy them at garage sales or thrift shops for $1 a plate. I do not need cups and saucers, or dainty bowls.

Grilled steaks are served on a set of western style plates with different ranch brands on them. You surely are not surprised that I have a set of dishes with ranch brands, are you!?

Mix your casual stuff with your more formal dishes and linens. Some people don't like to use china and crystal, especially with kids because it might break. Here's my thought on that possibility: If it gets broken or stained, get another one. If you can't get another one, find something close in design. If you can't find that, let it go! At New Year's Eve dinner one year, my grandson Hunter, who at the time was five years old, was upset that he spilled melted butter on a silver table runner. I told him that from then on, that runner would be the "Hunter Learned to Eat Lobster Table Runner." I still use it fifteen years later and I always tell that story. It's a sweet memory!

My additional questions each time are:

- What tablecloth and/or placemats will be used?
- Which napkins work with the tablecloth and/or placemats? When I serve something messy, I have no hesitation about putting a roll of paper towels on each table.
- Do you need napkin rings? When I don't have napkin rings that I think work with the linens, I use ribbon, twine, and the string off of hay bales, which I wash first!
- Where will you place the napkins—in the middle of the plate, to the left of the fork, or above the plate?

- What is your centerpiece? It doesn't have to be fancy—one of the pots of ivy in your house will be wonderful. Just don't use anything too tall because then your guests can't see each other. You can use fresh fruit on a cake stand, cuttings from pretty greenery in your yard, or a row of your grandmother's teacup collection with grapes, olives, cheese straws, whatever looks inviting and munchy.
  - From Betty Crocker's *Hostess Cookbook,* she offers this idea: Use fruits in a monochromatic combination, such as strawberries, apples, tomatoes, cranberries red grapes or plums.
  - My late friend, Janet Bliss Mello, always said, "Just use what's around you. And make it pretty and inviting." Of course, Janet could take a paper bag, fill it with a weed called Old Man's Beard, tie it with kitchen twine and make it look welcoming. She really did do that. Don't try it. My Mammaw Gracie used to say "You can't make a silk purse out of a pig's ear." Actually, Janet might have been able to accomplish that!

I embrace the philosophy of *Rustic Joyful Food*, whose creator, Danielle Kartes, offers this thinking:

You don't have to lead a life of extravagance, have the best of everything, matching china, or a big beautiful room for entertaining. . . to share. Money may be tight, the struggle very real and yet we can still find ways to love the people in our lives through simply feeding them.

Luckily, in prepping and serving a meal, no one is going to give you a score or time you like ropers experience. If any guests do that, don't invite those guests back!

Things will go wrong—they always do! It's okay! Ree Drummond, also known as The Pioneer Woman, was interviewed by *Cowboys and Indians* magazine and was asked about her best tips for entertaining. I appreciate her answer and realize that is one of the many things that makes her so appealing to us. She's just so authentic and encourages us to do the same for ourselves and our guests! She said,

It may sound counterintuitive, but I think the best approach to entertaining is to be OK with imperfection. In our social-media-driven world. . .the standards are set so high, for not just food, but also for décor, for the state of our homes, for everything. In reality if we want for everything in our environment to be perfect, we'll never have anyone over . . .

So, welcome imperfection, crazy mishaps, and keep reading because you'll find some BIG mishaps in my cooking history.

TIPS & HINTS

- This is one of my very best tips: take notes as you prepare a meal. For example, for Mike's 70th birthday, we had thirty-one guests, and I made too much food. I wrote things like this on the back of the menu:
  - Tomato—bought eight; used four
  - Onion—sliced three; had 1/4 of that left
  - Lettuce—prepped three heads; had half left over
  - Pg 6 of a recipe book—doubled it; completely gone. Put tomatoes in the center and spread guacamole around the tomatoes
- When I serve a Taco Bar, I like to try veggies not typically seen on a Taco Bar, such as thinly sliced radishes, jicama, hothouse cucumbers, or even a bowl of fruit which is usually berries. I'm always surprised at how many people add berries to a Taco Salad.
- If you don't set the table with the utensils and napkins and want to put them with the buffet items, put them at the *end* of the line. Guests don't need to carry their utensils and napkins as they create their salad.

- I like to make meatloaf a little more exciting on occasion by filling the loaf pan halfway, then inserting a couple of hard-boiled eggs, or layers of ham and cheese, or a layer of mashed potatoes. It's always fun for other diners to find a surprise filling inside the meatloaf.

- For holiday meals, keep your timeline and shopping list from year to year. Don't recreate it! Make notes and adaptations each year, but for goodness sakes, don't start over! Note in the photos below that we list guests, our menu, our shopping list, and our timeline of what to do the day before, the morning of, and as guests arrive. Each year, we review our previous planning notes, make changes as needed, but we are not starting from the beginning.

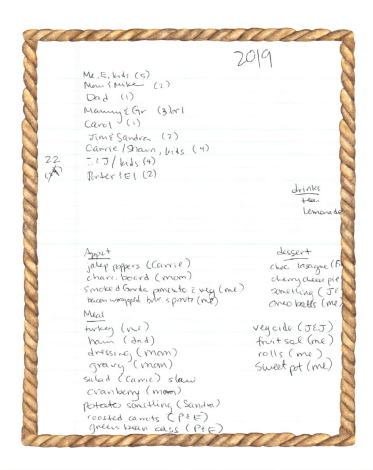

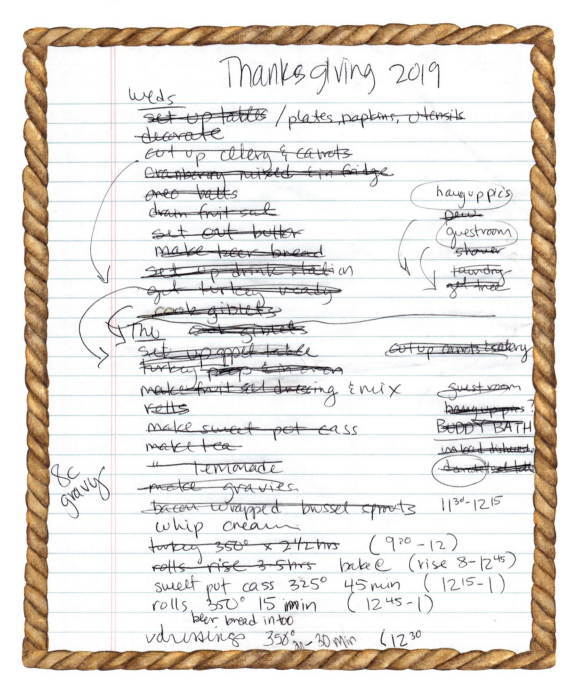

Thanksgiving 2019

Weds
- ~~set up table~~ / plates, napkins, utensils
- ~~decorate~~
- ~~cut up celery & carrots~~
- ~~cranberry mixed in fridge~~
- ~~oreo balls~~
- ~~drain fruit sal~~
- ~~set out butter~~
- ~~make beer bread~~
- ~~set up drink station~~
- ~~get turkey ready~~
- ~~cook giblets~~

~~hang up pics~~
~~pew~~
~~guestroom~~
shower
~~laundry~~
~~get tree~~

Thu
- ~~set up apple table~~   ~~cut up carrots & celery~~
- ~~turkey prep & in oven~~
- ~~make fruit sal dressing & mix~~
- ~~rolls~~
- ~~make sweet pot cass~~
- ~~make tea~~
- " ~~lemonade~~
- ~~make gravies~~
- ~~bacon wrapped brussel sprouts~~ $11^{30}-12^{15}$
- whip cream
- ~~turkey 350° × 2½ hrs~~   ($9^{30}-12$)
- ~~rolls rise 3-5 hrs~~   bake @ (rise 8-12^{45})
- sweet pot cass 325° 45 min   ($12^{15}-1$)
- rolls 350° 15 min   ($12^{45}-1$)
  beer bread in too
- ✓ dressings 350° 20-30 min   (12^{30}

8c gravy

~~guestroom~~
~~hang uppies?~~
BUDDY BATH
~~unload dishwasher~~
~~donate/sell table~~

Now it's time to:

- Mount your horse (create your menu),

- Nod your head and let the lineman know to let the calf out (make your list of groceries, your timeline and what you need for your table setting),

- Step off (do as much as you can prior to guests arriving, set your table and prepare your meal),

- Focus, focus, focus and visualize how much fun it will be to feed family and friends. . . even if things go wrong!

Chapter Two

Rope the Calf You Draw:
The Night of the Sliding Chicken

In spite of our quirks, it works. And if it doesn't work, it's usually funny. Then it becomes a story. And the story becomes a memory and that bonds us, too.

Becky Johnson and Rachel Randolph

Ropers plan for certain moves from the calf. When you get a surprise, you just have to adjust. Gail Hughbanks Woerner describes it this way in *Rope to Win*,

Once that gate is opened and the chase is on, anything can happen.

Remember the quote from Ree Drummond in Chapter One that things will go wrong? Ina Garten says the same thing in *Make It Ahead*. . .

when surprises happen—and they always do!

And may I just say, that when you really, really want to make a good impression, surprises will happen. A Sliding Chicken comes to mind.

When Mike and I were first dating, we invited his Sister Cousins and their spouses for dinner. Sue and Rodney Clayton came, but Kay and Clarence were busy that night. Kay and Clarence came on another occasion for a lovely candlelight dinner.

Sue and Kay are sisters to each other and technically cousins to Mike, but they were raised almost as siblings. Mike treats them as though they are his sisters and loves them with full accord. Thus, I have, without their permission but also without any protest from them, dubbed them The Sister Cousins, a capitalized title because it is a title of prominence and affection. I love their stories about their childhood and the aunts, Big Momma and other cousins. When we have Family Meetings, which consists of meeting for barbeque and very, very cold beer, we often relive the stories, and we all laugh as though it just happened. The three cousins start laughing, can't stop, and the cousins' spouses join in the laughter. Even our favorite waitresses laugh with, or maybe at, us. We always leave a nice tip, so they listen to us giggle.

One of my favorites is the story of Mike's late brother, Pat, and Sister Cousin Sue when Sue and Pat were about four years old. I call it *Sue and Pat Go for a Drive.*

Drive is a stretch of the term. In reality, they got in the car, with Sue sitting INSIDE the steering wheel to do the guiding. I can just see her with legs dangling from the steering wheel. Pat was underneath to push the pedals. They were pretending to drive and accidentally rolled out onto River Oaks Boulevard, which is a busy street in Ft. Worth. The car was parked on the curb facing away from River Oaks Boulevard. When Pat released the emergency brake, they began to roll backwards toward the highway. Fortunately, it was not a busy traffic time. The car, with Sue and Pat aboard, continued to roll backwards across two lanes of traffic and came to rest with the back wheel against the median curb. The story has it that Sue's mom came flying out of the house so fast to rescue them that she was almost airborne. I think they were not allowed to play in the front yard again until they were perhaps eight or maybe ten.

It may sound sort of mean to laugh about young children driving onto a busy street, but since no one was hurt, it has become a classic story. It's a miracle that no one was hurt. It could have gone so very wrong. There were five grandchildren who were raised almost as siblings as they lived very close to each other. Only three of the five are left. I think telling that story reminds them of their strong family connection, and how they were always in each other's yards and lives.

I especially relish in the recipes that The Sister Cousins share. One of my favorites is a recipe for Lemon Pudding Cake, which Kay and Sue's mom, Margaret, made for family celebrations. I make it routinely for family celebrations, church suppers, to take to friends who need a meal. If you need a meal, then you need a Lemon Pudding Cake.

♘ ♘ ♘

Lemon Pudding Cake - Doris Wdes

Margaret

1 Box Duncan Hines Lemon cake mix
1 bx Lemon instant Pudding
1 Bx Lemon jello
4 eggs
3/4 cup oil
3/4 cup Water
   Dump in bowl & beat 10 min Pour in
1 0 X 14 pan & bake 35 or 40 min at 350°

_____

        Topping - Do not cook.

1/2 box powd sugar - 1 3/4 cup

2 Tbs - oil

1/3 cup Lemon juice

   Mix tog. Punch holes in cake &
Pour topping over cake while hot.

Prettier

~~Pretty~~ in a Bundt Pan

Lemon Pudding Cake

Preheat the oven to 350°. Grease or spray with nonstick spray a 10" X 14" pan.

For the cake:

1 box lemon cake mix

1 box, small, lemon instant pudding

1 box, small, lemon Jello

4 eggs

3/4 cup oil

3/4 cup water

1. Dump all ingredients in bowl and beat 10 minutes.
2. Pour into prepared pan.

For the glaze topping (do NOT cook):

1/2 box (1- 3/4 cups) powdered sugar

2 tablespoon oil

1/3 cup lemon juice

1. Mix together while the cake is baking. You want it ready when the cake comes out of the oven.
2. Punch holes in the cake and pour glaze topping over the cake while it is still hot (see some options in **TIPS & HINTS**).

Now on July 20, when Sue and Rodney came for dinner, as you see listed on the menu, I was serving Roasted Chicken. Roasted Chicken is easy, so I was confident in serving that. There may have been early wine served, and when I went to get the chicken out of the oven, the chicken started sliding, and I caught it just before it hit the floor. Luckily, I was wearing oven mitts. I was really nervous and wanted to make a good impression on Mike's family. I made an impression for sure. You know that feeling when your back is turned to several people in the room and you can feel their stares? Luckily, someone laughed and then I joined in. Rodney especially loves to talk about The Night of the Sliding Chicken. It had to be turned into a funny story! I've often wondered what's funnier than a Sliding Chicken. I do know one thing that is at least as funny. Years ago, a friend told me about her first Thanksgiving turkey. She took the blue rubber band off the legs and stuffed the turkey. She then put the rubber band back on and put it in the oven. She always referred to it as the Thanksgiving with the Blue Butt Turkey. Yep, a Blue Butt Turkey is funnier than a Sliding Chicken.

I will say that the table setting for The Night of the Sliding Chicken was nice (shown on the title page)! Ambience rescued me.

Luckily, I have found a prevention for Sliding Chickens. I now use Ina Garten's recipe *Roast Chicken with Bread & Arugula Salad©* found in her book, *Make It Ahead.* It is a wonderful recipe both in taste and easy preparation, but the beauty is that it is cooked on top of bread. Bread prevents sliding chickens!

Another family favorite, which is usually made for dessert, but then serves as a breakfast bread, toasted and slathered with butter, is the Andersson/Bergman Family Gingerbread Cake. One of my favorite parts of making gingerbread is that it makes your house smell so good!

One of Mike's cousins wrote out the story of how this recipe got shared in the Bergman family. An aunt found the recipe in a box. It was written on the back of an envelope. The title of the recipe was *Great Grandmother's Gingerbread Recipe (over 100 years old).* The front of the envelope was dated May 10, 1957, which would date this recipe into the mid-1800s and was a part of the ancestry line of Ola and Berget Andersson, who settled in the Clifton, Texas area.

Andersson/Bergman Family Gingerbread Cake

Preheat oven to 350°. Grease or spray with nonstick spray a 9" X 9" pan.

<u>Wet mixture</u>

1/2 cup sugar

1/4 cup butter, softened

1/4 cup shortening

1 egg, whisked

1 cup molasses

1 teaspoon vanilla

<u>Dry mixture</u>

2-1/2 cups sifted flour

1-1/2 teaspoons baking soda

1 teaspoon cinnamon

1 teaspoon ginger

1/2 teaspoon cloves

1/2 teaspoon salt

1 cup hot water

1. Cream sugar, butter, and shortening.
2. Add whisked egg and molasses, mixing well.

3. To the wet mixture, add flour, baking soda, cinnamon, ginger, cloves and salt. Mix well.

4. Add hot water and beat until smooth.

Bake in 9 X 9 pan at 350°. Let it cool for about 10 minutes and serve warm. Many of the Bergman family members claim it is for an after-dinner dessert with ice cream on top. Other members claim that it is a breakfast food. Mike and I claim it is an anytime treat.

TIPS & HINTS

- I don't always roast whole chickens. If it's a meal just for Mike and me, I use thighs, bone in, skin on. We remove the skin after it's cooked, just to reduce fat consumption. But keeping the skin on and the bone in while cooking yields more flavorful and tender meat.

- When you poke holes in the Lemon Pudding Cake, use skewers (toothpicks are too small and will take you a long time to make enough holes), one in each hand and just go to town poking holes all over. These will make bigger holes and the glaze will soak in better. I work from the middle to the edges. If I need to, I use a brush to move some of the glaze that pools at the edges.

- I like to make the Lemon Pudding Cake in a Bundt Pan. I spray it with baker's spray—a mixture of oil and flour. It's really pretty and you can see the glaze topping dripping through the cake as you slice it.

Now it's time to:

- Mount your horse (create your menu),

- Nod your head and let the lineman know to let the calf out (make your list of groceries, your timeline and what you need for your table setting),

- Step off, which is *not* the same as jumping off (do as much as you can prior to guests arriving, set your table and prepare your meal),

- Focus, focus, focus on the gift of having a family favorite and the stories it creates!

Chapter Three

Cowboys Need Their Coffee and Pie: Don't Show Up without the Family Favorite!

Admit it. We've all hidden our favorite food from our family at least once.

Gracie, Jody/Mom, Paul

There are some items included in every meal on a ranch. The cook, often called *Cookie*, prepares coffee that is so strong a cowboy might close his eyes and brace himself for a rush of dark, hot, and thick liquid. The first gulp is a signal that the day has begun.

Mike's friend, Dusty, introduced us to Ken Beck and Jim Clark's book, *The All-American Cowboy Cookbook* which offered this option:

> *Here's a recipe for cowboy coffee: Take a pound of coffee, add water, boil for half an hour. Throw in a horseshoe; if it sinks, add more coffee.*

I haven't tried that method! Probably won't! Further proof of the sanctity of coffee for a cowboy comes from Grady Spears and Brigit Binns in *Cowboy Cocktails,* as they claim that

> *For a cowboy on the open range, coffee was like life's blood. Breakfast, lunch, dinner, and just shootin' the breeze—all were accompanied by steaming hot coffee no matter what the weather.*

Do you have a specific formula for making your coffee each morning? We do. It is half Community Coffee Dark Roast and half Starbucks French Roast. I once thought it would be important to have a fancy coffee pot. I was moving into a new house and would have an office with coworkers in my home. I determined that keeping office workers happy started with good coffee. I read reviews, asked my friends, and settled on a pot that had a thermal carafe. It was recommended by a cooking show, giving it five out of five stars. Yes indeed, I was getting a winning tie-down coffee maker! It should do everything for you, because it cost $300!

To make perfect coffee, beyond your preferred formula, the instructions said to preheat the carafe by running hot water into it. That's easy enough, except that although my kitchen is very close to the water heater, it takes an interminable length of time to get hot water. I hate to waste anything, especially water. Therefore, I keep a pitcher under my kitchen sink, and when I need hot water, I capture the cold water in the pitcher, filling it until I feel heat. I set it aside and save it for watering plants. The water still was not hot enough to heat the carafe. A Pyrex glass measuring pitcher to the rescue! I filled an eight-cup pitcher with water, heated it in the microwave, poured it into the carafe to preheat the thermal vessel for a few minutes. Next, I poured the water back into the Pyrex pitcher to let it cool off and use it to water plants. So far, I do not have any coffee. But I do have two pitchers of water to provide a drink for my plants.

So much for fancy coffee makers. I donated that coffee maker to a university office kitchen. I am reminded of this cowboy adage, "Didn't see that bull coming."

For my family, a holiday meal, no matter if it's the Fourth of July, Thanksgiving, Christmas or Cousin Sam's birthday, there will be The Cherry Cheese Pie. I learned the Cherry Cheese Pie recipe from a neighbor whose name is long forgotten. I made it the first time in May of 1973 and it has changed, like all of my recipes, through the years.

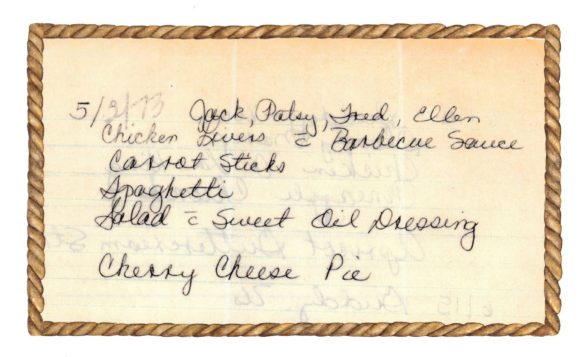

As I look at this menu, I am baffled as to why I thought Fried Chicken Livers with BBQ sauce would be a good appetizer. I think that sounds just awful, but it is making me laugh now. A positive thought is that I must have always been an adventurous cook, but when you overdo your strength and go too far out there. . .yuk! In this case, I went past adventurous and slid through the dirt into downright reckless. At least I made a winning tie-down recipe by serving a delicious dessert. Surely that made up for a terrible choice for an appetizer!

Thus, began an almost fifty-year romance with The Cherry Cheese Pie. I've served it with Spaghetti, Lasagna, Grilled Sirloin, Oven-baked Grecian Rib Eye Steaks, Tuna Cheese Melts, Beef and Vegetable Stew, Ham and Cheese Stuffed Meatloaf, Chili (with NO beans in Texas, WITH beans in other states), Taco Salad and Stuffed French Loaf Sandwiches. There's more, but you get the point: The Cherry Cheese Pie is a winner no matter what else is served!

About ten years ago, no one had mentioned the pie in a while, so I made something else. OH MY GOSH! My children, Gracie Westbrook Packwood and Paul Westbrook are loving, funny, accomplished and well-educated adults. They are both really good cooks! They are married to adorable spouses, Eric and Juli, and have given us grandchildren who are cuter and smarter than yours. I'm pretty sure you would argue with that declaration!

All of those wonderful traits of my children vanished when I arrived without The Cherry Cheese Pie. I was ultimately forgiven and have, since that day, made sure I appeared at every holiday meal with The Cherry Cheese Pie!

The Pie has been served to so many guests! I've served it to church groups, book clubs, visitors from near and far, my Policy and Decision-Making class from a university, Curriculum Audit Teams, to my parents, my brothers and their families.

One notable guest enjoyed The Cherry Cheese Pie on February 15, 1990.

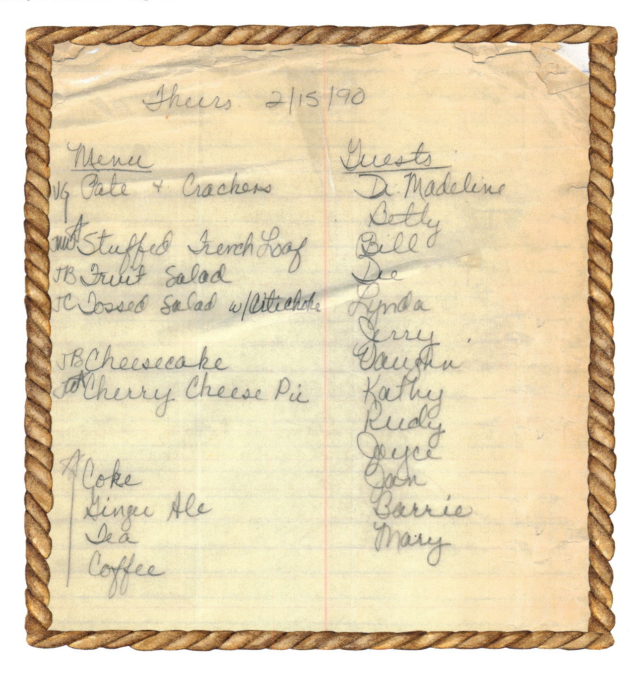

Theirs. 2/15/90

Menu   Guests:
VG Pate + Crackers   D. Madeline
                              Betty
      Stuffed French Loaf   Bill
JB Fruit Salad   Dee
JC Tossed Salad w/Artichoke   Lynda
                              Jerry
JB Cheesecake   Vaughn
   Cherry Cheese Pie   Kathy
                              Rudy
                              Joyce
                              Jan
   Coke   Barrie
   Ginger Ale   Mary
   Tea
   Coffee

The late Dr. Madeline Hunter was a professor of educational administration and teacher education at UCLA. She developed what came to be known as *The Lesson Cycle.* It was a direct instruction program that was implemented in thousands of schools and school districts throughout the United States. She influenced hundreds of thousands of educators to make instruction better for children.

Dr. Hunter was in great demand as a keynote speaker and a trainer, not only in the United States, but internationally as well. Despite her notoriety, she was an unassuming and modest woman.

I had contracted with Dr. Hunter to teach the principals and other administrators in the school district where I was Director of Professional Development. During one of our previsit conversations, just on a whim, I asked her if she would like a home cooked meal with a small group of admirers.

"Oh yes!" she blurted out. She elaborated, "I get tired of airplane food and room service meals." And so, the planning began. This had to be a great menu, planned down to the last minute and full of fun!

The guest list was limited to twelve people who vowed to not tell any of our peers as everyone was an admirer of Dr. Hunter and would have loved to be in her company.

My favorite part of the evening occurred when someone asked, "Dr. Hunter, would you like some more wine?"

"I would!" she exclaimed as she jumped up from the table, retrieved the wine and went around the tables, refreshing each person's glass. The esteemed author of twelve books, over 300 articles and seventeen instructional video tapes also had a heart to serve others. What a role model!

Dr. Hunter loved The Cherry Cheese Pie and asked me for the recipe, later writing me a very warm and personal note for the hospitality.

By now, you might be hoping I'm going to share the recipe and here 'tis!

The Cherry Cheese Pie

Preheat oven to 350°.

1/2 cup butter, melted

1/8 teaspoon salt

2 tablespoons sugar

1 cup flour

1 (21 ounce) can cherry pie filling.

1 (6 ounce) bar cream cheese, room temperature

1 egg, room temperature

1 teaspoon vanilla

1/3 cup sugar

1. Mix the melted butter, 1/8 teaspoon salt, the 2 tablespoons sugar and the flour and press into an 8-inch tart pan (9 inches will work, but it is a tad too big).
2. Pour the cherry pie filling over the crust mixture.
3. Use your electric mixer to blend the cream cheese, egg, vanilla and 1/3 sugar until it is creamy—no visible lumps.
4. Carefully spread the creamy mixture over the cherries. Be careful not to let the cherries bleed into the creamy mix. To prevent this, I dollop the cream cheese mix in several spots, then carefully connect them.

Bake at 350° for 25-30 minutes, just until it starts to lose its sheen. Let it cool 30 minutes and enjoy it warm and runny or refrigerate a few hours and serve it cold.

Make The Cherry Cheese Pie ASAP!

TIPS & HINTS

- If you're serving an appetizer with cream cheese, save the Cherry Cheese Pie for another time. You don't want to serve multiple items with the same bold ingredient.

- When you are measuring sticky ingredients, such as honey, molasses or jellies and jams, spray your measuring cup with nonstick cooking spray. The ingredients will slip right out. It is especially helpful to spray your spoon or spatula when stirring chocolate as you melt it.

Now it's time to:

- Mount your horse (create your menu),

- Nod your head and let the lineman know to let the calf out (make your list of groceries, your timeline and what you need for your table setting),

- Step off, which is not the same as jumping off (do as much as you can prior to guests arriving, set your table and prepare your meal),

- Focus, focus, focus on cooking with friends!

Chapter Four

Team Roping with the Header and the Heeler: Cooking with Friends

If you really want to make a friend, go to somenone's house and eat with him . . . the people who give you their food give you their heart.

Cesar Chavez

Cooking with friends is a lot like team roping. Team ropers are two competitors who each have an assignment: one ropes the head; the other ropes both back feet. The cow is released immediately. Team ropers practice together, and they practice when apart. They can switch roles because each person has practiced doing both sets of skills needed. They trust each other, have fun with each other and offer grace when a mistake is made.

Team roping requires practice, and so does cooking with friends. The goal is to produce a meal and enjoy it together. What makes it successful is organization and assigned roles, unless you've done it so long you have a rhythm together. Some of my favorite moments are cooking in someone's kitchen or a friend joining me to cook in mine.

Many of the friends I've cooked with through the years are part of a group of Texas educators who came together to learn more about leadership. All of us had been trainers for a statewide leadership program.

The group that gathered initially in 1991 has continued to meet once or twice a year, long ago switching our focus to topics other than the leadership training. We've studied Peter Senge's *Fifth Discipline*, David Whyte's poetry, *The Art of Play* by Stuart Brown, and other compelling topics. Our setting is a nature-filled and serene locale, often a Bed and Breakfast. We take turns facilitating the topic to be studied for the session. We share meals and luxuriate over each morsel. We have shared stories from meals. We collectively grumbled over having Peach Cobbler that only had one bite of peaches. We bring bottles of wine, put them on a table and share and share alike. After all these years, we are extended family. We call ourselves The Star Learners as we are all ravenous learners—and diners, too!

Through friendships nurtured in Star Learners, I get to be a part of other shared retreats and gatherings where we team up to cook and dine. The *Cook and Write* retreat, designed and facilitated by two Star Learners, Beverly Charles and Lyn Mefford, offers an opportunity to share recipes, write stories, cook, and eat. The food is always tasty and beautiful, but I must say, the stories—oh, the stories!—make me laugh, smile, cry, celebrate and rejoice!

At our *Cook and Write* retreat in 2017, Beverly and Lyn invited us to submit recipes according to the theme, *Memorable Recipes from Around the World*. A fantastic and tasty recipe story was submitted by my dear friend, Terry Morganti-Fisher. At the retreat, Terry talked about her grandfather's recipe for Capellini that included anchovies, tomatoes & capers. She shared a love for the dish with her paternal grandfather, and the two of them enjoyed it on Christmas Eve as part of the Feast of Seven Fishes; other family members, not so much!

Although we wanted the recipe, Terry explained that her family of origin just made up recipes as they went along, and none of it was in written form. She referred us to a recipe by Lidia Bastianich, in *Lidia's Family Table,* that is very similar to what her family served.

Terry is more than a treasured friend; she is my Sister of Choice. We have worked together, played together, served on two professional boards together, and found the best restaurants in every city we've visited. Sometimes we meet halfway between Ft. Worth, where I live, and Austin, where she lives. We go to a snazzy hotel, take more clothes than anyone needs for an overnight trip. We take food, wine, cute things we've found that we think the other one needs. She lives an intentional and joyful life. If she's your friend, what you say, do, or feel is safe. One hundred percent safe. Sometimes she tries to stifle a giggle, but she can't, and it comes out as a captivating laugh! I love the laugh and the person who delivers it with Italian gusto!

All four of Terry's grandparents were immigrants from Italy. The sauces they made took about a week to complete, and just hearing that makes me want to go start a pot of Bolognese Sauce. Terry's story of making pasta with her Grandpa was divine! She captured our attention and our hearts with her story. Grandpa Morganti made pasta dough without ever measuring any ingredients. He would shout out what he needed— "FLOUR!" "EGGS!"—to Terry's Grandma, and the feisty, but tiny, woman scuttled about to deliver the goods. She doesn't sound feisty running back and forth delivering ingredients on demand. But here's how I know she was feisty. At a typical multi-course family dinner, wasps began swarming and drifting into the dining room. The men went outside, all about studying the nest, pondering what to do, when Grandma Morganti appeared through a third story window with a shotgun, blew the nest up and ordered everyone back to the table.

Terry told us how her Grandpa rolled out the pasta dough on the kitchen table topped with a large Formica covered cutting board. He rolled out the pasta intended for Ravioli—thin, with wide ribbons—with a broom handle. After adding the filling, putting on a top layer of pasta, cutting and crimping them into ravioli size, Terry and her sister ran them into a bedroom, where a clean bed sheet had been placed on top of the bed for the drying of the pasta. That's how "ravioli on the bed" got its name. Picture two little girls running back and forth spacing the pasta out just so when they reached the guest room. How charming is that?! This was the second course of often a six or seven course meal because as Grandma Morganti said, "Ya gotta eat!"

I have also enjoyed being part of what we called The Fab Four, made up of my friends Linda O'Neal, Lyn Mefford, our mentor, the late Shirley Hord, and me. We took turns hosting annual retreats in our homes. The hostess designed the menu and had ingredients with recipes and assigned roles ready to be put into action. We did not pick up a burger from the corner fast food diner; we made an elegant meal together. The hostess also selected a book for us to read prior to gathering and designed art activities and reflective questions about our book. The Fab Four members have prayed for, and over, each other, made jewelry together, painted Matryoshka dolls from Russia, hunted on Facebook for a long-lost love of one member, hunted seashells, and ridden a golf cart through the woods behind my house.

Shirley was twenty years our senior and was one of the most quoted researchers in the United States on the topic of *Change in Education*. She was a meticulous researcher, succinct speaker, and an extremely independent and modest human. We sadly said goodbye to Shirley when she passed in October of 2019. Lyn, Linda and I continue to gather to cook, eat, learn, and support each other. I think we have collectively prayed for each other and each other's families for hundreds of hours through the years. Being friends with Lyn and Linda is an adventure, a warm part of my heart and offers support beyond belief.

In April of 2010, I was hostess to The Fab Four and had selected the book, *I Heard the Owl Call My Name* by Margaret Craven. I discovered this book while working on my doctorate. Since the setting of the book was the Pacific Northwest, I really thought that we should have a menu that reflected foods from that area. I was only modestly successful because I wanted to serve salmon, which I do not eat, so we had Cornish Hens and steamed green beans.

Food Date 4 (4/4/10)
Hor D'urv

Meals   Fab 4   Snacks
                                red bell
Thurs   celery
    ~~Mexican~~   rye crkers
                                seedy crkers
Fri: cereal, yog, fruit   ~~hummus~~
lunch   tea   Hens salmon ~~cheese~~
Dinner: ~~Pork Chops~~ ~~tomatoes~~ fruit
         ~~salad~~ grn bns
         Beer Bread

Sat   bkd french toast   Desserts
Brk { bacon   tiny bundt
        bld yr own yogur parfait cakes

lunch   Lyn
dinner   Mezza Luna
Sun   Dorothy's Egg

Linda Oneal
Lyn Mofford
Sherly Hord

As we talked about our book, I highlighted for The Fab Four a charming story told in our book about the óolachon fish. The author described it this way:

Every year, in late March, the tribe prepared for the coming of the óolachon, the candlefish, a season so deep in the tradition of the people that all the taboos and superstitions were remembered and followed. No pregnant woman must cross the river. No body must be transported upon it. The chief of the tribe must catch the first fish.

The night before the run of the óolachon, a great feast was held, and during that time, the chief related the first myth of the óolachon. The óolachon fish is affectionately called a candlelight fish because of the legend that claims that the fish is so oily, one can dry it and then light it with a match and the fish serves as a candle. I haven't tried it and you shouldn't either. Just because a cowboy wryly offers, "Ride this bull. No one's ridden him yet," does not mean it's a good idea.

I've told the legend of the óolachon fish to many people. I convinced Shirley and another friend to dine with me at the First American Restaurant in Vancouver. I only knew what I had read in a travel magazine. As we cautiously walked down the steps to a basement, they paused, demanding to know if I knew where we were going.

"Yes," I said with fake confidence, "We are going on an adventure." It was an adventure with a charming meal, ambience, and First American dishes. We ordered a Fisherman's Platter, and I queried the waiter if it had óolachon fish on the platter. The face he made was enough answer for me!

The waiter elaborated that óolachon fish are mostly oil and the grease is separated and used in other ways. I had to ask, you know I had to ask, "Have you ever tried to light an óolachon fish with a match and use it as a candle?" Again, the face he made was enough answer for me! Let me repeat what I said earlier, just because someone says you can do something doesn't mean you should try it.

The general practice of The Fab Four was that the hostess assigned four roles for meal preparation:

1. The Chef, who was the hostess,
2. The Sous Chef, who followed the lead of the Chef—chopping, sorting, stirring, mixing as needed,
3. The Table Setting Designer and member of the cleanup crew, and
4. The Head of the Clean Up Crew.

For that Fab Four gathering, we made one of my favorite breakfast casseroles, Dorothy's Eggs.

Dorothy's Eggs

Preheat oven to 325 °.

12 eggs, whisked until blended

34 ounces of canned, cream-style corn

4 cups (1 pound) grated cheese (I use Extra Sharp Cheddar)

1 tablespoon Worcestershire

1 (8 ounce) can chopped green chilies, drained

Salt to taste

Pepper to taste

1. Whisk all ingredients; pour into a 13 X 9 baking dish which has been sprayed with nonstick spray. This much can be done up to 24 hours in advance. If you opt to do this, let it sit out and come close to room temperature before baking.
2. Bake for 1 hour and 15 minutes until it is firmly set.
3. During the last 15 minutes, check every 5 minutes to prevent over-browning. See extra notes in the **TIPS & HINTS** section at the end of the chapter.

Dorothy, of *Dorothy's Eggs*, was the mom of one of my very long-time adorable friends, Karen Nicholson, known to me as KJ. KJ and I are Kitchen Buddies. She is married to Jim and they have adult daughters, Jamie and Jody. I refer to them as the Nicholson Mojos because we can put a meal together, paint a room, pack a house, run a lap or two, and then enjoy an adult beverage—all in one day. I love all of them dearly. If you spend time with anyone of the Nicholsons, you will laugh about something, nothing, and everything, and you will learn something that makes you a better person.

The first Nicholson menu appeared on July 14, 1981 and at this writing, the most recent menu appeared on September 23, 2019. There was a visit scheduled for 2020 and I am confident that you know what happened to that visit.

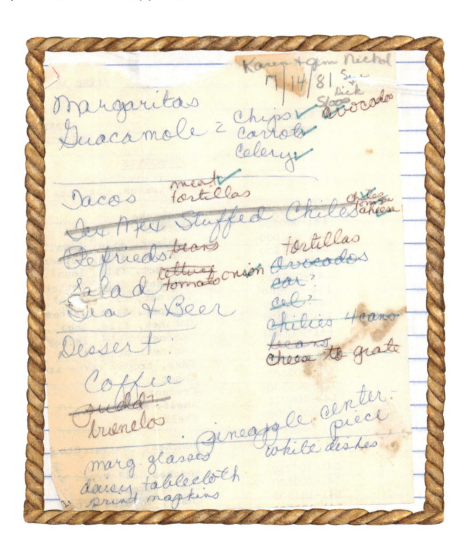

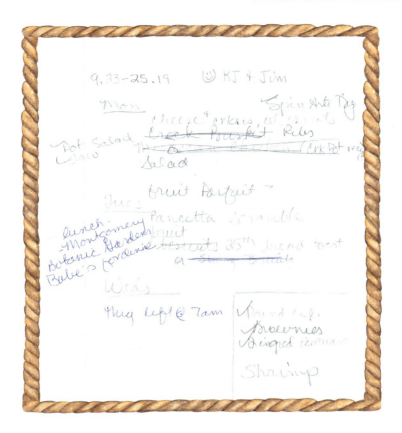

KJ and I have been Kitchen Buddies for close to forty years. We haven't lived in the same city since 1982, so our visits have occurred a few times each year. Sometimes the weekends have been planned weekend fun, or "I'll be in town for a conference. Is your Guest Room open?" Or, "I'm attending a Board Meeting. Is your Guest Room available?" We've stayed in each other's houses for weddings. More than one of those weddings was mine. All of those visits included time in the kitchen.

We've helped each other pack up to move and unpack and settle into a new home—multiple times! We've even stayed in each other's houses when the host and hostess were out of town. The arrangement was, "Here's where you'll find the key. Enjoy the kitchen, reset the air conditioning, and lock up."

There is not one favorite meal or menu that we have made, but we always have a new recipe to try. Among the first words we say as we enter each other's home is, "What are we cooking?"

It has happened more than once that the hostess set out a recipe for the visitor to review and prepare to make, and the visitor proclaims, "Oh this looks great! Let's be sure we copy the recipe."

At that point, the hostess laughs and says, "I got this from you ten years ago," which makes us laugh like crazy. There's nothing better than making memories as you make good food. In this case, our memories slipped!

One of the "I Got It From You" recipes is Rachael Ray's "Double Dumpling Chicken Stoup" found in *Rachael Ray Recipes online.* Karen introduced me to that hearty, full-of-flavor chicken meatball stoup in 2010. Rachael says that stoup is thicker than soup, but not as hardy as stew, thus it is stoup! It's brimming with veggies, fresh cheese, and best of all, a hint of freshly grated nutmeg. The nutmeg gives it an earthy aroma. Pair it with a crusty bread and YUM!

I make this stoup often, partially because it's as good as eating a dessert and partially because it has gnocchi in it. I prepare no other recipe with gnocchi, yet I really like gnocchi. I've made this for many dinner guests and multiple families in times of need; friends or church members whom I may or may not know who have lost a spouse, parent, or child; friends who have had surgery, and for a family member whose house burned.

I've liked every recipe from Rachael Ray that I've ever cooked, and I appreciate her opinion on following diet trends and fads. In *30-Minute Get Real Meals*, she advises us to enjoy really good carbs in moderation, but to not abandon hearty pastas and sammies for tasteless "low carb" cardboard fake pasta. She explains it this way:

> *Bottom line: Eat fewer carbs and maintain a better bottom, waist and everything else. But, do not go to such extremes that you deny yourself and those who eat with you to the point of damaging your relationships, your own personality and possibly your health. Try eating fewer carbs and moving more and I bet you'll feel as good as you look for as long as you like!*

TIPS & HINTS

- I routinely put chilies or peppers in casseroles and soups. When I have guests that I think will not want chilies, I divide the casserole in half, putting chilies in one pan but not in the other. For soups, I serve chilies and peppers as a garnish for diners to design their own heat!

- When possible, I use fresh spices. For example, in any recipe that calls for nutmeg, I grate a nutmeg seed. Yes, one can just grab a can of the spice and I have, on occasion, done that, but the fresher the spice the better it tastes!

Now it's time to:

- Mount your horse (create your menu),
- Nod your head and let the lineman know to let the calf out (make your list of groceries, your timeline and what you need for your table setting),
- Step off, which is *not* the same as jumping off (do as much as you can prior to guests arriving, set your table and prepare your meal),
- Focus, focus, focus on the gift of cooking with kids! It's fantastic and messy!

Chapter Five

Start Kids Roping on a Post, Not a Calf: Cooking with Kids

Cooking with kids is not just about ingredients, recipes and cooking. It's about harnessing imaginations, empowerment and creativity.

Guy Fieri

Tie-down ropers come in all shapes, sizes, ages, ethnicities, and with many languages. In all those variations, there seems to be a universal belief among ropers, at least that I've met, that no matter how young, if kids show an interest in swinging a rope, it is wise to nurture and guide that interest. It's considered wise because it is a way to teach the importance of safety, etiquette, discipline, and skill.

I've heard it described it this way:

You don't want them practicing on their brother, sister or the dog. Whatever you do, don't start them with a real calf. Start out using a short tree, a T-Ball stand or a fence post!

The same philosophy works with cooking. Invite your kids into the kitchen to help at an early age. Pre-schoolers can ice cupcakes, which will be imperfectly perfect. They can dump in premeasured spices and slosh an already cracked egg into a mixture.

Writing this during a pandemic has prompted me to notice one bit of advice for teaching young cooks. It seems to be a long-standing recommendation that we teach kids to wash their hands!

We shouldn't be surprised that hygiene has been important for many, many years! I read this in *Kitchen Fun: A Cook Book for Children*, which was published in 1932. My Mammaw Gracie gave it to my mother for Christmas in 1934, when she was eleven years old. Their advice on the inside cover includes:

Wash your hands.

Put on your apron.

From my first cookbook, *Betty Crocker's Cook Book for Boys and Girls,* published in 1957, they offer an entire page of kitchen practices which includes this tip:

Wear an apron to keep your dress or blue jeans clean and be sure to wash your hands.

The T. Colin Campbell Center for Nutrition Studies offers guidelines for different age groups, starting with toddlers, the 3-5 year old cooks, the 5-7 year old cooks, the 8-11 year old cooks, and 12 years old and above. For every group, there are two important factors to consider:

Their physical ability to do the task and their mental ability to comprehend the task and, in particular, the possible dangers involved.

My children, Paul and Gracie are miracles! I was a very young, uneducated, and self-centered person when they arrived. They are Irish twins, siblings born less than twelve months apart. I was just barely twenty-one when Paul arrived, and Gracie was born on my 22nd birthday. I often say that they turned out to be not only functional, but fabulous in SPITE of me, not because of me. I was immature, and I grew WITH them, BECAUSE of them, and FOR them. They inspired me to become a better person. I'm grateful for the grace they give me for my early rocky parenting.

Gracie and Paul grew up as toddlers thinking that everyone's mom needed to study. I finished my bachelor's degree when they were in the first grade, my master's when they were in the eighth grade, and we all graduated in May of 1988, the two of them from high school and me with a doctorate degree.

Like most preschoolers, Gracie and Paul wanted to help in the kitchen. I let them chop bananas with a butter knife, encouraging them to be so careful as though it was a sharp knife. Yes, it was messy!

I would have enjoyed using the internet resources available today when I was a young mom, wanting to teach my kids to cook. A practical reminder from *frugalandthriving.com* offers that we should remember these four guidelines:

- Go slow,
- Teach hygiene and safety,
- Accept that there will be a mess,
- Use regular utensils.

I appreciate these suggestions, and I offer another viewpoint about kid size utensils. The author points out that kid utensils are expensive, kids outgrow them quickly, and those extra utensils just add to the clutter. I do think kid size utensils are fun and provide a sense of ownership to children. I see these utensils frequently in thrift shops for cheap prices. I enjoy kitchen clutter.

While they were in elementary school, Paul and Gracie participated in a cooking class through the local newspaper. There were weekly instructions and recipes. Their favorite, as well as mine, was The Week of the Crepes.

Paul would whisk the batter, getting all the lumps out and pour the batter in the preheated, eight-inch skillet, with butter just about to sizzle. Gracie would swirl it around so that the edges were thin. Paul would turn them out onto kitchen towels to dry and the process would begin again. When the crepes were cool, they would then stack them into three or four layers, with a variety of fillings. For one stack, they spread cream cheese with cherries. I'm sure it was cherry pie filling. It was so pretty to see the thin, soft, golden crepes with bright red cherries and cream cheese dripping down the sides.

The next adventure during The Week of Crepes was Strawberry Banana Rolled Crepes. They used frozen strawberries, probably because all of the trimming work was done for them, and probably because the frozen version was cheaper. For this concoction, they began by squirting whipped cream on each other's heads. They did a lot of things to each other's hair when they were kids. One of my favorite stories was when they were two and three years old. They were outside, playing with Gracie's doll and dipping the doll's hair into a mud puddle. They were having so much fun and I thought there was no harm in it. After all, we could wash the doll's hair. HA! Not so fast, momma! I looked again and they were dipping their own heads in the mud puddle. Our family was soon gathering for the 47th Annual Mason Fourth of July Backyard Shindig. Off to the bathtub for Paul and Gracie!

When back on task after the hair fun, Paul and Gracie laid the crepes out flat and squirted a more or less straight line of canned whipped cream and placed sliced bananas inside. They then folded the crepe over, made a zigzag line of whipped cream on top of each crepe, then layered strawberries on the top of the whipped cream.

I recall that the whipped cream was runny and knew we should have used real cream that we whipped ourselves. Remember that they were in elementary school, just learning and not serving their creations to guests. In fact, they consumed them, with a little help from me, as fast as they made them.

The Week of The Crepes ended when I insisted that they make either Savory Spinach and Mushroom Crepes or Sausage Crepes. They were not having anything to do with spinach, and that's my fault. I was raised on canned spinach, canned asparagus, and canned carrots, even canned tamales. I didn't even know what fresh vegetables tasted like until I was well into my thirties.

If I were teaching them to make Spinach Crepes today, I'd search the internet for recipes and find something that combined sautéed mushrooms, garlic, fresh spinach and some Herbs de Provence, add goat or feta cheese, roll them up, sprinkle more cheese on top and bake until the cheese was melted. YUM! I may look for a recipe like that tonight.

Beginning in the sixth grade, Paul and Gracie were expected to cook one dinner each week. Gracie liked to use Hamburger Helper and presented it with lettuce, which was our salad. Paul liked to serve us a can of SpaghettiOs. I encouraged both of them to venture out and follow a simple recipe. Their meals were not always delicious, but neither were mine. The meals were always edible and they learned their way around a kitchen early.

If you're thinking how smart that idea was, it was actually self-preservation for me. I was principal of an elementary school with about 800 students, served on a statewide board studying school finance, and was in the early stages of working on my doctorate. I was overwhelmed and figured it was a win-win. Two nights a week, I didn't have to figure out dinner and they assumed some responsibility and learned some new cooking skills. I was functioning with the belief that I could multi-task, but the brain research says we can only rapidly shift from task to task. Or on the ranch, the cowboys would say,

A lot of horses are saddled, but you can only ride one at a time.

One of our favorite stories from this era was about a crockpot. This was early in crockpot cooking and most crockpot recipes had ingredients swimming in a sea of cream of mushroom soup, or cream of celery soup, or cream of anything soup. The meats looked anemic, unless we browned it in another pan first, but it was all edible.

One morning, Paul asked who was responsible for dinner that night, and I replied, "I am and it's already cooking." Picture a 13-year-old boy, with a pitifully distorted and disgusted face. With that face you just conjured up, Paul slurred his words and offered his disdainful opinion via a question, "Eww, is it in the crockpot?" I doubt that I thought it was funny that day, but the memory of his face looking so terrified by food from the crockpot makes me laugh.

What's especially funny about that story is that now Paul and Juli own at least eight crockpots, often using five or more at the same time for large gatherings. They will have two with chili, one version is very hot and the other one is milder; two will have queso dip, again one very hot and one milder, and a stew of Paul's design. One of my favorites from their crockpot recipes is the chunkiest, thickest, most flavorful queso you will ever have. If you make it, serve it with sturdy, large chips. It is not for fragile chips! Make it for the next crowd you have over. They will forever LOVE you!

Paul never makes it the same way twice, but the following recipe is the starting point. I follow the recipe as written, minus the hatch chilis, which are not available year-round. Paul and Juli buy a big supply when in season and freeze them so that they always have access to the heat!

Queso (Hot!)

1 pound ground venison or ground beef

1/2 to a whole Sweet Texas Onion, chopped

1 tablespoon Fiesta Brand Uncle Chris' Seasoning

1 (2-pound) block regular Velveeta brand processed cheese

1 (8-ounce) block cream cheese

2 (10-ounce) cans Rotel brand tomatoes and chilies

1 quart of whole hatch hot green chilies (already roasted – see Tips & Hints)

1 tablespoon Julio's Seasoning, more to taste

1 tablespoon Fiesta Fajita Seasoning, more to taste

1 (13.4-ounce) can diced pickled jalapeno (about 15 slices)

1 (7-ounce) can of green enchilada/salsa verde sauce

1. Brown the venison/beef with chopped onion.
2. Add all additional ingredients, stirring to mix.
3. Here are options for heating:

* Place the mixture in a crockpot on low 2-3 hours before serving, or
* Place the mixture in an aluminum foil pan, cover with foil and put on a smoker on indirect heat.

If you want more heat, use Hot Rotel and more jalapeno slices.

Paul is an excellent cook and loves to plan and feed crowds of people. His annual Paul's Crawfish Boil is quite the popular event. He uses many crockpots for that event. His other very popular dishes include Venison Roast, Stew, and Gumbo. He makes two versions of Gumbo, one with his preferences and one with Juli's preferences.

Paul's preferred Gumbo includes oysters, crawfish, shrimp, dove, duck, chicken, sausage, fresh okra and boudin. Juli's preference is just sausage and chicken.

Paul is also a real professional diner, a person who LOVES to find out of the way and unusual restaurants. He will likely know the owner and the manager, and they will know him. He reminds me so much of my dad in that wherever he goes, he knows someone, and they know him, and it's often related to food.

Gracie, too, is an excellent cook and probably delivers a meal each week to a homeless shelter, a children's home, a family in need or just to surprise someone. Oh! If you are Gracie's friend and you have a baby, count on a meal from Gracie.

One of the dishes for which Gracie is best known is her Chicken Pot Pie, which is so full of vegetables you might not notice the chicken in it! It's a huge pie and probably can feed a family of four for a couple of nights. Her other famous dish is Laura's Grandma's Sugar Cookies. Think of perfectly shaped cookies, such as bells, Christmas trees, stars, with a thick strand of icing around the edge and a thin layer of icing on top. They are pretty enough to hang on a tree. They glisten and taste like you can take a bite and let it melt.

Chicken Pot Pie

Preheat oven to 350°.

<u>Crust:</u>

4 (9 inch) deep dish frozen pie shells (unless you make your own pie crusts—good for you!)

<u>Filling:</u>

1/2 cup butter (8 ounces; 1 stick)
1/2 - 3/4 cup chopped sweet yellow onion
2-4 cloves of garlic, chopped or smashed
1/2 cup flour
1 teaspoon salt
1 teaspoon pepper
3 cups chicken broth
3 tablespoons cream cheese, cut into small cubes
2 cups chicken, chopped, shredded or cubed into bite size pieces
2 teaspoons Herbs de Provence spice
16 ounces package of frozen mixed vegetables, cooked and drained

1. Prepare 2 pie shells by browning them for 5-8 minutes at 350° and allowing to cool before filling.
2. Bring the other 2 crusts to room temperature to use on the top of the pies.
3. Saute onion in butter until softened (about 3-5 minutes), stirring often.
4. Add the garlic and saute just until fragrant, less than one minute.

5. Blend in flour, salt and pepper.
6. Gradually whisk in broth and continuously stir until bubbly and thick.
7. Add the cream cheese and stir until it is melted into the sauce.
8. Stir in the chicken, Herbs de Provence, and the vegetables. Keep blending this mixture until all is incorporated.
9. Pour into the two browned shells.
10. Top with the second crust and seal the edges. Make it special by fluting the edges. That means pinch them between your thumb and finger and make a little fold. Mine never look perfect, but they look good. Cut 4-6 slits in the top crust.

Bake at 350° for 30- 40 minutes, depending on how golden brown you like the crust. Serve warm.

I think it's funny that both Gracie and Paul have some organizational habits that I use. All of us put out Post-it notes when we serve a buffet indicating what dish goes where. That way, we ensure that there is room for every bowl, dish, basket and tray. Also, when guests arrive, we don't have to remember to take everything out of the refrigerator and oven. I may have taught the Post it note strategy to them; I may have learned it from them.

For Paul's 50th birthday dinner, he requested the menu shown in the picture dated 8.11.19. We had family, extended family, and a couple of friends as our guests. Note that Paul's menu included Mike's Drippingly Delicious Ribs, which take hours to cook on indirect heat on the smoker. If you remember The Cherry Cheese Pie, you know it was on his wish list.

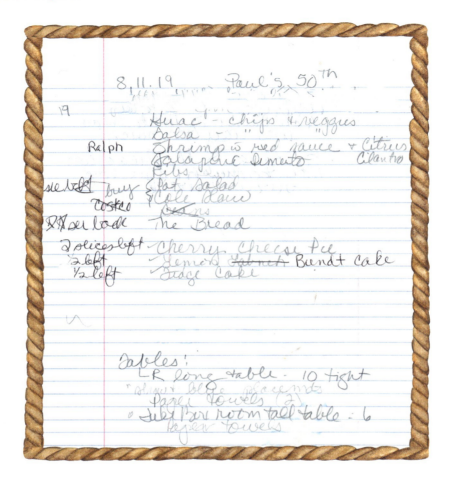

To decorate for this special dinner, I put out tall place card holders with pictures of Paul from birth through adulthood, plus some of his school papers from first and second grade. The table was set with white pottery plates and heavy navy-blue napkins. When serving ribs, one needs sturdy plates and napkins. I also put rolls of paper towels on each table! Now, you might be thinking that would look way too casual, and it does. However, your guests' comfort is important and they will appreciate being able to totally enjoy the messiness of ribs with a sauce. To offset the sturdy look, I put out colorful metallic sprays and spread glitter across the table. They were small in size, because I wanted Paul's pictures and schoolwork to be the focus of each table.

It was so much fun to answer questions about the pictures and hear people's comments, "How cute!" "How old is he here?" "He and Gracie looked like twins when they were little!"

Paul's birthday parties while growing up were usually all about sports, hunting, and lots of friends. At one of his birthday parties, my dad asked, "How does he know all these kids?" What's ironic about that is that my dad was the same way. If there were people around, he knew them, invited them over if he didn't know them, and called the new friends the next day to invite them back.

Gracie's 50th birthday dinner looked very different for two reasons. They have very different personalities, and hers occurred during the pandemic, necessitating a small group. She wanted sea scallops and a spinach salad. I used the recipe for Layered Spinach Salad from my aunt's files, whom you met in the Prologue. You know, *Sister!*

07.27.20   G's 50TH!
       Gra's birthday
Packwoods, Laura, Kelly & Casey
       Mike & me

Mon @   - Central Market Charcuterie Bds
noon   w Crackers
               add Burrata
          - ~~First House Salad~~ 24 hr
          - Tuscany Sea Scallops

          - Bread

          - Pound Cake
    &   -   Fondue Fountain

A Favorite Recipe: _Layered Spinach_

Salad —

1# fresh spinach torn
into bite-size.

2 hard-boiled eggs,
chopped, 6 green onions, sliced,
10 slices bacon, cooked +
crumbled, 1-10-ounce pkg. frozen
thawed, 1/2 ounce carton sour
cream, 1/2 cup mayo or

From the Kitchen of: _____ Serves: **OVER**

---

salad dressing, 1/4 teasp. lemon
pepper seasoning, 1/8 tsp garlic
powder, 1/2 cup grated Romano
cheese (optional)

Layer spinach, eggs, green onions
bacon, + peas in this order in
bowl. Spread mayo mixture over
top ingredients covering to edge of
bowl. Sprinkle w/cheese, with
cheese. Cover, refrigerate 2-8
hours. Toss gently before serving

Sister's Layered Spinach Salad

Fresh spinach torn into bite size pieces, about 1 pound

2 hard boiled eggs, chopped

5 green onions, sliced

10 slices bacon, cooked and crumbled

1 (10 ounce) package of frozen peas, thawed

1 (8 ounce) carton sour cream

1 cup salad dressing, such as mayo or Miracle Whip

1/4 teaspoon lemon pepper seasoning

1/8 teaspoon garlic powder

1/2 cup grated Romano Cheese (see options in **TIPS & HINTS**)

1. Layer spinach, eggs, green onion, bacon and peas in a large deep glass bowl (mine is 11 inches in diameter).
2. Combine sour cream, salad dressing, lemon pepper and garlic, sealing to the edge of the bowl (that means spread out this mixture to the edge).
3. Put the cheese on top, cover and chill for 8 hours.
4. Toss gently before serving.

Gracie's house is bigger than mine, and we could spread guests apart for appropriate distancing, so I hosted at her house. I took all the ingredients, my favorite pans, and yes, one was a crockpot! I took placemats, napkins, napkin rings, my china, eight small vases of hydrangea flowers and a partridge in a pear tree. It took three days to get it all back to my house, but it was a grand celebration.

I decorated the tables as I did for Paul, putting out pictures of Gracie from birth, through school, her wedding portrait, at her medical school graduation, and as a mom. Because of the limited number of guests we could invite, we had her family, Mike and me, and three of Gracie's closest friends. Those friends, Laura, Kelly, and Casey, are Gracie's Sisters of Choice. Watching the four friends laugh and enjoy each other's company, I had a flashback to Gracie's thirteenth birthday. She wanted to make funnel cakes with her friends. I agreed and set it all up. There were no accidents, and everyone, except for me, enjoyed making the cakes. But during the party, I wondered about my judgment to let a group of thirteen-year-old girls stand over hot oil and make their own funnel cakes. It was stressful that day; today, it's a sweet memory.

Most pleasing to me is that all of our grandchildren know their way around a kitchen. Paul's children, Hunter and Addie, and our bonus grands, Juli's daughters, Jane and Gwen, have developing degrees of skill and interest in cooking. One of them said it's just important to know the way to the kitchen!

When I taught Hunter to make spaghetti sauce at about age ten, he took some home to his parents, and declared, "This is the very best spaghetti sauce I've ever made." Of course, it was the only spaghetti sauce he had ever made, so he was technically correct! Addie always wants to make something with cheese or something sweet—brownies, a pie, a cake, snickerdoodles. . . yeah, me, too!

Gracie's children, Mason, Camden and Libby, can make meals, cookies, and know how to grill. One of my favorite memories of Mason and Camden was when I moved into my current house, which is literally through the woods from their house (but not over a river). The boys were seven and five years old. They prepared a picnic lunch, complete with peanut butter and jelly sandwiches and lemonade, grabbed a blanket and appeared at the door to serve lunch to everyone helping me move in. They had, at that young age, already learned that preparing a meal and serving was an act of love. Today, I can get their attention by saying, "Shrimp is served," and Mason will appear. For Camden, I say, "Queso is served."

Libby and I make bunny shaped cakes every Easter, dying coconut to be the green grass, putting little cinnamon candies to shape a mouth and a tiny piece of raisin for the eyes. Actually, we use whatever we can find to decorate the bunnies, and that results in a perfectly imperfect product!

All ten of the Bergman grands have helped in the kitchen. One Christmas, I made individual servings of ranch dressing and let the little ones insert celery, carrot and cucumber sticks. Yes, we spilled a few, and it was no big deal. Everything wipes up easily! Of course, I used plastic cups so there was no broken glass. Broken glass does NOT wipe up easily.

TIPS & HINTS

- If you buy kid size utensils at a thrift store, just be sure to run them through the dishwasher on hot water—twice—before you hand them over to your little ones.

- The kid's cookbooks I mentioned are still available and have been reprinted many times. I think that newer cookbooks for children offer healthier options.

- Some options for the Layered Spinach Salad include slicing your eggs instead of chopping them. I think the sliced ones look elegant. I often substitute plain yogurt for sour cream as it has less fat! For the cheese on the top, I've read some options and have used some of them. Instead of Romano cheese, I've used slices of Swiss cheese, freshly grated parmesan cheese and grated Italian cheese blend. Some recipes for layered salads include a sprinkling of sugar with the sour cream mixture and suggest that it should be refrigerated for 24 hours.

- If I were a mom to young children, I would want to follow the example of Amy Nelson Hannon. In her book *love, welcome, serve,* she quotes 1 Peter 4:8-11,

Above all, love each other deeply, because love covers over a multitude of sins. Offer hospitality to one another without grumbling. Each of you should use whatever gift you have received to serve others, as faithful stewards of God's grace in its various forms . . . so that in all things God may be praised through Jesus Christ . . .

Amy describes how that verse impacted her.

Love deeply. Welcome gladly. Serve faithfully. So that in all things God may be praised through Jesus Christ. These three words captured my heart: Love. Welcome. Serve.

Now it's time to:

- Mount your horse (create your menu),
- Nod your head and let the lineman know to let the calf out (make your list of groceries, your timeline and what you need for your table setting),
- Step off, which is *not* the same as jumping off (do as much as you can prior to guests arriving, set your table and prepare your meal),
- Focus, focus, focus on the gift of being able to cut corners as you prepare a wonderful meal!

Chapter Six

A Wrap and a Hooey Will Save You Some Time: Not Everything has to be from Scratch

I became stirred on the inside about encouraging and equipping folks to embrace hospitality— intentional kitchening—so people wouldn't miss one more minute of the love that happens when they make and serve food to their people.

Amy Nelson Hannon

After a roper flanks a calf (picks it up and lays it down on the ground oh so very gently), he/she decides to wrap one time or two times prior to the Hooey (the Hooey is the half hitch that locks your tie together). Two wraps take longer but is safer in that it is more secure. However, one wrap saves a short amount of time, and it's risky, but it may allow you to win, which means money!

Sometimes as a cook, you need to just do one wrap and let it fly! You can heat and eat, and that's not palatable. Or you can make everything from scratch, which takes a really long time, depending on what you're serving, of course. So here's what I've learned: make an important part (or maybe two parts) of the meal from scratch and take short cuts on the rest! One of my favorite chefs, Ina Garten, says,

> *I'm a big believer in buying things. Use the resources around you. If you know a food store that makes a fantastic potato gratin, work with that and build around it. I've been saying this for twenty years—your friends won't have any more fun if you make everything yourself.*

My older brother and my husband's boss came for dinner on September 18, 1973. I wanted to impress both guests. The boss was from New York City, and we lived in Memphis at the time. Being raised in Texas and now living in the South, I really only knew southern dishes.

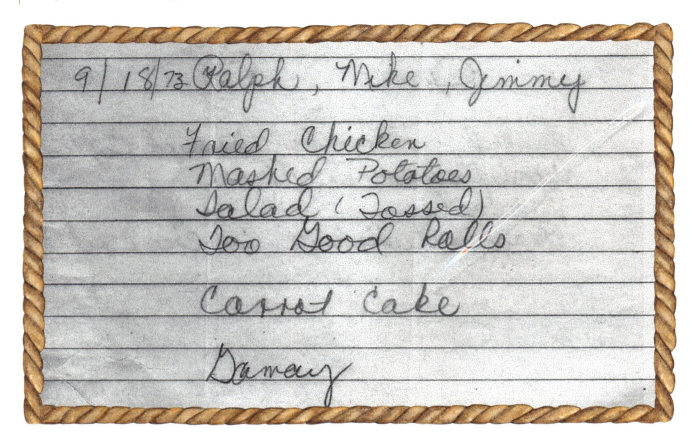

9/18/73 Ralph, Mike, Jimmy

Fried Chicken
Mashed Potatoes
Salad (Tossed)
Too Good Rolls

Carrot Cake

Dorinda

Even though I had two small children, who were three and four years old at that time, I thought I had to make everything from scratch.

Think about how much time I must have spent cutting up a whole chicken, shaking it in a paper bag with flour, salt, and pepper, and then frying 3-4 pieces at a time. It reminded me of a scene in a movie, *Always,* with Holly Hunter playing Dorinda. Dorinda, who is preparing a dinner for a new romantic interest, wants to make a good impression, so she throws flour all over herself so that it looks like she has really been working at fixing the dinner. I looked like that character when I was shaking the chicken in a paper bag and it tore open. I was wearing navy-blue bell-bottom pants and the flour was so obvious on those navy-blue pants!

As if the process of homemade fried chicken wasn't time-consuming and messy enough, I made homemade mashed potatoes. In those days, I boiled whole potatoes with the skin on, let them cool a little, peeled them completely and then used a hand mixer. I still have that hand mixer! It's a wonder that I didn't burn it up with all the work it has done through the years. It's a lot of preparation to fry a chicken AND make the mashed potatoes. You have to combine the potatoes with butter, cream, salt, and pepper. It's so good, you'll be happy you did it! Homemade rolls, of course, were a must. One can't serve the boss and your esteemed older brother packaged rolls! My neighbor and friend, Sarah, gave me a recipe called Too Good Rolls. She was just a year older, but about 10 years more experienced in the kitchen than I. She grew up in Kentucky, but had lived in New York City for a while, so I thought she was so smart and sophisticated and glamorous. She had long dark hair and deep brown eyes, and when she gave advice, I listened carefully. She offered the recipe called Too Good Rolls, and shared with me this wonderful tidbit of information, "You don't even have to let it rise." I was such an inexperienced cook that I didn't even know bread had to rise in the first place, but I nodded knowingly, as though I was greatly relieved.

Too Good Rolls appears on many menus up until 1983. Its last appearance on a menu was Mother's Day of 1983. When I started looking at my menus and old recipes to write this book, I found the recipe and decided to give it another try. How it fell off the radar in 1983 is a mystery. It appeared again for Thanksgiving 2019. The 2019 version was quickly consumed and declared, "dense, delicious and buttery." These are NOT light, fluffy rolls. They are wonderful in the winter with hot soup. Caution: if you cook them one or two minutes too long, you will be able to use them for batting practice.

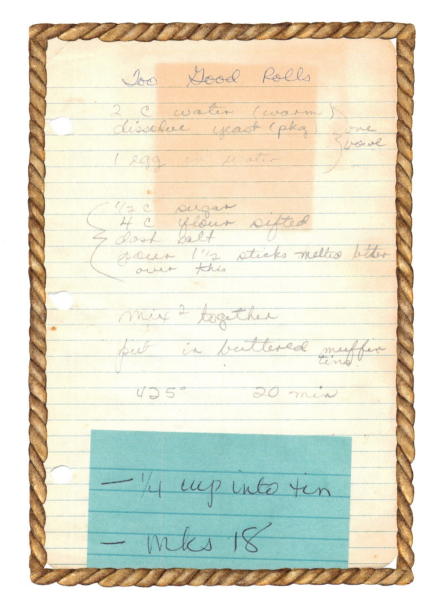

Too Good Rolls

2 c water (warm)
dissolve yeast (pkg)   } one
                        } bowl
1 egg in water

½ c sugar
4 c flour sifted
dash salt
pour 1½ sticks melted butter
over this

mix together

put in buttered muffin tins

425°   20 min

— ¼ cup into tin

— mks 18

Too Good Rolls

Preheat oven to 425°. Grease or spray muffin tins with nonstick spray. It will make about 18 rolls.

Wet mixture

2 cups warm water
1 egg, lightly whisked
1 yeast package

Dry mixture

1/2 cup sugar
4 cups sifted flour
Dash of salt

12 tablespoons (1 and 1/2 sticks, 6 ounces) butter

1. Dissolve the yeast in the warm water until bubbly then lightly stir in the egg.
2. In a separate bowl, stir the sugar, flour and salt together and pour the melted butter over the dry ingredients.
3. Mix the wet and dry mixtures together.
4. Spray your scoop with nonstick spray so that the mixture will release easily. Scoop ¼ cup per roll into muffin tins.

Bake at 425° for 20 minutes.

There are so many ways to save time! Some people like to get chopped onion in the produce section of their supermarket. I actually enjoy chopping my own vegetables. It's a satisfying tactile moment to chop my onion in uniform little white squares. I should say almost uniform. I feel that way about celery, carrots, potatoes, and other vegetables. I draw the line at butternut squash. I go straight to the chopped version in the produce aisle and/or the frozen food aisle.

Not only can you get chopped onion in the produce aisle, bags of chopped onions are available in the frozen food section. You can also find Mirepoix, which is typically a combination of onions, carrots and celery, the base of many soups and casseroles. I've not tried any of these frozen options, but I have many friends and family who swear by them.

Some supermarkets offer shortcut options in their deli. I like to buy skewers of mozzarella cheese, grape tomatoes, and olives. Artisan bread is readily available and a huge time-saver. My favorite shortcut is to get one of the beyond beautiful cakes or cupcakes from the supermarket bakeries. I'll buy one of those to save my time and energy when I am making a more elaborate entrée. That is true unless someone in my family expects The Cherry Cheese Pie.

TIPS & HINTS

- As an extension of Ina Garten's advice to use resources around you, I like to get a Charcuterie Board from a local market, transfer what they assembled onto my wooden tray and add other delicious treats. For example, the market puts only meats and cheeses, so I add a basket of fancy crackers, a small pot of Apricot Conserve, two types of olives and almost anything else in the refrigerator that looks like it should be on a Charcuterie Board.

- Don't assume that everyone loves steak, or chicken or anything else. I often serve an entree salad with separate bowls of protein options. People can pick any, or all, or none for their plate.

- When I invite guests for a meal, I email them and ask, "What food allergies do you have AND what do you absolutely not eat? For example, I do not eat fresh tomatoes. I don't care how good your momma grew vine-ripened tomatoes. I WANT to love them, but I do not. So, please let me know which foods you cannot or will not eat."

- Instead of getting flour all over you and the countertop, put a piece of wax paper or aluminum foil out on your countertop. Measure your ingredients over it and let it catch the spills! That makes for a quicker cleanup! Being eco-friendly, remember that aluminum foil can be recycled over and over. Wax paper will decompose.

Now it's time to:
- Mount your horse (create your menu),
- Nod your head and let the lineman know to let the calf out (make your list of groceries, your timeline and what you need for your table setting),
- Step off, which is *not* the same as jumping off (do as much as you can prior to guests arriving, set your table and prepare your meal),
- Focus on how much fun it will be to feed your family and friends, unless they stay too long!

Chapter Seven

That Pasture has been Overgrazed: Guests Are Funny and So is Food

The only healthy way to live life is to learn to like all the little everyday things—like a sip of good whiskey in the evening, a soft bed, a glass of buttermilk, or a feisty gentleman like myself.

Gus McCrae

To begin each day on a ranch, the Ranch Manager tells the Straw Boss what needs to happen that day. The wranglers take care of the horses and the cowboys take care of the cows. Cows have to be moved from pasture to pasture so that they don't stay too long and overgraze the pasture, much like two of our guests, who stayed way too long.

On December 1, 1974, a couple came for dinner and almost stayed for breakfast. My husband and I, with our two children, lived in a modest apartment with bedrooms upstairs and a living room, large kitchen, and breakfast area downstairs, along with what polite company calls a powder room. I'm not sure what cowboys might call it and honestly, I don't think I want to know.

Our guests stayed and stayed and stayed. They stayed until 2 am. Up until midnight, I would go to the kitchen and bring out more crackers, cheese and olives. After midnight, I ceased my food service. When one of them would get up, we kept thinking that they were getting ready to leave. Nope, they were just going to the restroom and would emerge, sit down and just keep talking. One of them would occasionally go outside and when that first happened, I thought they were warming up their car to leave. Nope, they were smoking outside. At least they were outside and not smoking in our apartment.

I wonder what in the world we talked about. Memphis State University (now University of Memphis) was in the national championship playoffs in 1973 and perhaps we were reliving that success, or predicting what the next season would hold. The season lasted from March 10 to March 26, and MSU lost to UCLA. Perhaps we were grieving that loss, albeit many months later. Maybe we were watching Christmas movies.

We had very young children who would be up the next morning in their footed pajamas and messy hair, wanting to watch cartoons on our old box TV, which was the size of a Volkswagen. They would want to have a bowl of sugary cereal. Why I ever thought sugary cereal was good for my kids, I don't know. Any cereal that has multiple colors of red, purple, yellow, green, and blue is questionable. But it's good for two reasons. It tastes yummy and it keeps young children happy on Saturday morning.

We don't remember how we knew our guests; we just remember that they wouldn't leave. Maybe the meal was so good that they wanted to stay for leftovers. At lunch. Now it's funny, but I doubt that it was funny that night. It's funny that they were so oblivious to common sense. It's funny that we were such dimwits that we tolerated it.

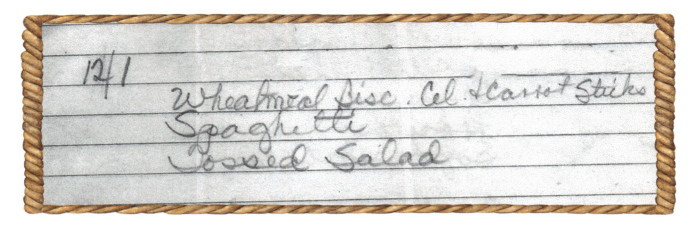

12/1

Wheatmeal Disc. Cel. & carrot Sticks
Spaghetti
Tossed Salad

For that meal, and many meals after that, I made my standard spaghetti sauce. When you serve a hearty spaghetti sauce over noodles, you don't need much else. Looking at my collection of menus, spaghetti sauce was listed many, many times as the entrée, and I served a light appetizer, such as a veggie tray with some cheeses, a tossed salad and a dense bread. The dense bread is terrific for sopping up leftover sauce. In those days, I followed a spaghetti sauce recipe from a comprehensive cookbook.

A friend called several years ago and asked me for the recipe. I told her she had it in her cookbook. So, we opened the cookbook and I started talking, saying things like, "Oh, I don't do that. I use both butter and olive oil now." Or "Oh, I changed how much garlic, meat, brand of tomatoes . . ." Finally, my friend, in great frustration, stopped me and said, "So far not one thing is the same as the recipe. Please rewrite this recipe as you make it now!" Through the years, the recipe morphed into this version:

Spaghetti Sauce

3 tablespoons olive oil

1 tablespoon butter

6 slices bacon, each slice cut into four semi-equal pieces (I trim the fat off)

2 onions, chopped

1/2 pound sliced mushrooms

4-6 cloves of garlic

1 pound ground beef or venison

1/2 pound ground hot or sweet Italian sausage

1/4 teaspoon whole nutmeg, grated (I don't actually measure it)

1 (28 ounce) can Italian plum tomatoes, mashed with an old-fashioned potato masher

1 (6 ounce) can tomato sauce

2 tablespoons sugar

4-5 tablespoons of Italian seasoning

A few fresh basil leaves, torn into small pieces

Salt and freshly ground pepper

1. In a large stockpot, warm oil & butter over medium heat and sauté bacon for 2-4 minutes; remove the bacon pieces and save for another use (baked potatoes for tomorrow night's dinner?), add the onion and sauté until onion is translucent.
2. Add sliced mushrooms, sauté 4-5 mins.
3. Add garlic, sauté until fragrant, 30-45 seconds.
4. Add the beef/venison and sausage; brown the meats until no longer pink. To ensure uniform cooking, I get two spatulas, and I separate the chunks of meat as they brown. It's a good workout for your triceps.

5. Drain the fat off (see two options below)

6. Add the nutmeg. I do not measure the nutmeg; I just scrape the bean across a fine grater until I see a dusting of nutmeg and smell the aroma.

7. Add tomatoes, tomato sauce, Italian seasoning, sugar, salt, and pepper.

8. Let this simmer very gently, 1-3 hours—the longer the better. Stir frequently and add water—see **TIPS & HINTS** below!

I like to serve this over our favorite BOLD pasta as this sauce is too dense for "delicate" pasta such as angel hair or thin spaghetti. But I also serve it over spaghetti squash or zucchini noodles—less carbs, but seriously, it's so good over pasta! Perfect sauce for lasagna!

Use parmigiano-reggiano cheese—get a block and grate at the table.

I have so many menus where I've served Spaghetti! The appetizer needs to be light since the entrée is bold and heavy. I also often serve a side that is light. Some of my favorites are steamed asparagus, or skewers with mozzarella balls, olives, marinated artichoke hearts and tomatoes. As noted in Chapter 6, these skewers can be purchased in the deli of many supermarkets. I've also skewered marinated mushrooms and roasted Brussel sprouts (that was not a popular choice). On occasion, I've simply served burrata cheese with olive oil and balsamic vinaigrette with a chiffonade cut basil on top.

If my family are the guests, the choice is The Cherry Cheese Pie. I hope you read Chapter Three, "Cowboys Need Their Coffee and Pie." Other guests probably get a lighter dessert such as Strawberry Ice, a sherbet with a light cookie or a fruit compote layered with light whipped cream.

I also think families have the funniest names for some foods, and some really funny, maybe even odd, combinations. My dad used to always open a can of peaches when we had pizza. I wish I knew how that got started. There is no cultural tie and they don't particularly complement each other. Imagine my embarrassment when, at age ten, I went to someone's house for dinner and they served pizza without peaches. I asked if we were having peaches. Can you picture how they looked at me? The parents were polite and offered to get some peaches from the pantry. The kids roared with laughter. You are wondering if I outgrew that habit. No.

Sometimes foods get funny names by accident. My grandparents started a July 4th back yard tradition when my dad was a baby, around 1922 or 1923. Like many families, everyone brought something to share with the others. As I recall, people just claimed what they wanted to bring and everyone agreed. One aunt brought a loaf of white bread year after year. She did not bring any butter, or jelly or anything else to spread on it, she just brought a loaf of bread.

My grandmother brought potato salad that she worked on for two days. She claimed that the potatoes had to be boiled, peeled, and while they were still hot, have a few tablespoons of white vinegar poured over them. She elaborated that the potatoes had to be hot or they would not absorb the tanginess of the vinegar. I have no scars, but I did burn my fingers many, many times as I happily helped her make her famed potato salad. That dish should have received a new name of Hot Potato Salad, or perhaps the Finger-burning Special!

The little children played games such as Chase, Hide-and Go-Seek or sometimes Freeze. The often wanted to play on the swings, but the teenagers occupied the swing sets until someone made them move so that the younger children could use them. I remember two or sometimes three tables of men playing dominoes and women in lawn chairs talking about what happened on what they called their "Shows." As I listened to them talking one summer, my grandmother related a story about someone named Laura who ran off with Stan. I was shocked. I thought she must be talking about relatives that I didn't know. I asked whose cousin or aunt Laura was, the group of aunts, grandmothers and mothers all laughed. "No," my grandmother explained, "they are people on my television show."

When I was in high-school we had a foreign exchange student living with us. Juba was from Guatemala and joined our annual July 4th Backyard Shindig. One of neighbors made a tart slaw which consisted of julienned vegetables soaked for about three days in red wine vinegar, salt and pepper. It will make you choke if you swallow too much of the so-called dressing. It will make your eyes water if you take a big bite. As Juba took his first bite, indeed his eyes did water and he exclaimed, "That is very. . . It is Very. . . It is SO VERY . . ." and stopped mid-sentence searching for an appropriate word.

He stopped trying to think of the right word and asked, "What is the name of this?"

All of the teenagers shouted, "It's VERY!" And to this day, we still serve Very and tell the story of how it got its name.

I think most families have their favorite food which was renamed by a child's mispronunciation. Gorilla Cheese comes to mind. I am pretty sure that all small children like grilled cheese sandwiches. One of my children started calling that sandwich Gorilla Cheese when they were about two years old. I think that is such a lovely visual. I picture a large gorilla walking around passing out cheese sandwiches to little kids, none of whom are afraid of the gorilla.

I was known to make up names and songs to encourage my children to try new foods. I probably read most of these and adopted them immediately. For Broccoli & Rice Casserole, it was renamed Cheese and Trees and suddenly became the best food ever to Paul and Gracie. They liked peanut butter in celery with raisins atop the peanut butter and said it looked like ants sitting on a hill. That did not sound appetizing to me, but they liked it and used that term for years. I would love to learn what your family has as a favorite renamed food.

TIPS & HINTS

- If I'm cooking spaghetti sauce on the stove top, I let the sauce simmer for 1-3 hours, stirring often and adding water as needed.

- I often make this in a multifunctional cooker with a slow cook option. This appliance has many functions—sauté, simmer, as well as the slow cook option. I let it cook on low for 6-8 hours, again adding water as needed.

- The step of draining the meat mixture is an extra step but that removes lots of fat and the flavor is better. Here are two options:

  - Get a 9 X 13 casserole pan, line it with newspapers with paper towels on top of the newspapers. Spoon all of the meat mixture into the pan. Don't try to dump it all at one time. You'll regret it. Then, with a slotted spoon, spoon the meat mixture back into the pan. Carefully (it's hot!) dump into the trash the mess you just made in that casserole pan.

  - If you don't want to do all of those steps, I have been known to put on my rubber gloves, wad up paper towels and press the meat mixture, soaking up most of the fat. Two warnings: that's a lot of paper towels, and you are sticking your hand into a very hot pot.

- I still play around with the meat mixture. Sometimes I use 1 pound of ground pork, 1 pound of ground beef, and the sweet Italian sausage. I'll add wine and/or cream and let it cook down. That supposedly makes the sauce bolder.

- I've followed other recipes that add grated carrots, and other veggies. I'm neutral about the difference that makes, but some of my family likes it much better that way. I think that they just like to use the word, "Bolognese."

- When I empty the cans of tomatoes and tomato sauce, I swish a little water in them to capture the last little bit of juice and to prepare them for the recycle bin. I keep the biggest can on the counter, near the pot of simmering sauce and I pour all of the water from the various cans into the biggest can. I use that if I think I need a little extra moisture—it captures all of the juices!

Now it's time to:

- Mount your horse (create your menu),

- Nod your head and let the lineman know to let the calf out (make your list of groceries, your timeline and what you need for your table setting),

- Step off, which is *not* the same as jumping off (do as much as you can prior to guests arriving, set your table and prepare your meal),

- Focus on whom you can serve and support and how to receive that love and support when extended to you!

Chapter Eight

Reach Out to a Cowboy that's Down: The Methodists Are at the Front Door

Pimento cheese might just be called the most Southern dish on earth. Pimento Cheese has been dubbed 'the paste that holds the South together.'

Gayden Metcalfe and Charlotte Hays

It happened eight feet in front of me. Tommy was in the box, nodded his head, roped the calf, stepped off and as he moved to tie the calf, the jerk line in his belt did not release. Tommy went down to the ground, on his back, and the horse did its job of backing up, dragging Tommy through the dirt. The horse is supposed to back up to keep the rope tight to control the calf's movement as much as possible.

No fewer than twenty men rushed to help. Maybe there were just ten men; it could have been thirty men for all I know. Some stopped the horse from backing up, others released the calf, and some were ready to cut the rope holding Tommy. I was sitting with Tommy's wife, Diane, who was very calm. Diane's calmness was not indifference. Diane is a very level-headed human and not prone to overreacting. Her ability to stay calm is based on years of rodeo experience. More importantly, Diane has a knife in her pocket should she have to climb the fence and cut a rope. That's preparation! Tommy got up, brushed himself off and said, "Oops."

One of the things that struck me about this scenario was the response of the other ropers. Right there. Immediate action. Help the cowboy who's down.

These same ropers are competing against each other and it doesn't matter who wins, they reach out to shake the hand of the winner.

Methodists are a lot like that. We reach out to help someone who's down, and we reach out to congratulate those who have achieved a goal, accomplished a feat, or received recognition. With food. Methodists are famous for serving food, transporting food to someone in need or to someone who deserves a celebration.

If I'm ever lucky enough to meet you, ask me how long I've been a Methodist, and I'll be able to tell you in years and months. As of this writing, I've been a Methodist for thirteen years and two months. I'm a better person because of becoming a Methodist. Being a Methodist has introduced me to witnessing a human's capacity to offer grace, love, service and forgiveness.

I have had the honor of attending The Leadership Institute at the United Methodist Church of the Resurrection led by Pastor Adam Hamilton in Leawood Kansas. If you want to expand your understanding of faith, read any, or all, of Pastor Hamilton's books. At the Institute, I met and talked with an Exoneree, Pastor Darryl Burton, who spent twenty-four years in prison for a murder he was not involved in in any way. In telling his compelling story, he talks about the promise of redemption, the hope we have available, and how forgiveness was given to us and how we must forgive others. I ponder how a person can be wrongfully convicted, imprisoned for twenty-four years, and can forgive those who prosecuted and convicted him. He has created a foundation called Miracle of Innocence to help others wrongly convicted. I was honored and humbled to stand next to him and to thank God that Darryl is a model for love, hope, forgiveness and compassion. If you think you have been wrongly blamed by a friend or family member, read Darryl's story, which will help you put your story in perspective.

I also heard the heart-breaking story from Mindy Corporon, whose son and father were murdered by a shooter at a Jewish synagogue in Overland Park, Kansas. In an interview shortly after the shooting, she said, People keep asking me why I'm so strong. I'm strong because I have family, I'm strong because I have faith. I know that God did not do this. I know that there are evil, evil actions."

Determined to make something good come out of this tragedy, she and her family have created the Faith Always Wins Foundation, whose mission is "to promote dialogue for the betterment of our world through kindness, faith and healing." If you think you are entitled to judge others whose beliefs are different than yours, be it political, spiritual, or any number of differences, go read Mindy's story.

There are so many things I love about being a Methodist. Did I mention food? When it comes to food, there are protocols and traditions to follow if you are a Methodist.

My first Methodist church was New Fountain United Methodist Church, a small and charming country church in Quihi, Texas. Quihi is eight miles from Hondo, Texas; Hondo is forty-one miles from San Antonio. When I lived in the area, Quihi had four structures: one house, two churches, and the Quihi Gun Club, which twice a month becomes a Dance Hall. Don't picture a boozy, sleazy place. Picture an old wooden structure including the uneven and well worn floors, being enjoyed by moms and dads teaching their little kids how to boot scoot.

At New Fountain UMC, you will find the best people in the world—loving, unassuming, honest and smart. I must mention that their food is sometimes insidious. You think it's delicious, so you have more, not really knowing how dangerously addictive it is.

When there's a gathering at the church, there's always a potluck or a spread. There is a very important question during the planning process. It's not *if* there will be Pimento Cheese Sandwiches and Apricot Cookie Bars. It's *who* will be bringing those items.

There is an unspoken expectation of how these comfort-giving, love-producing creamy pimento cheese sandwiches will be made and presented.

Pimento Cheese Sandwiches – Basic Recipe

8 ounces yellow sharp cheddar cheese, grated

8 ounces white cheddar cheese or monterey jack, grated

4 ounces pimento, drained and chopped

1–1 ½ cups of mayonnaise or salad dressing, such as Miracle Whip

Salt to taste

Pepper to taste

1. Stir with a fork (or use electric mixer for a creamier texture) all ingredients.
2. Spread the pimento cheese mixture on one slice of bread; top with another slice of bread.
3. Cut the crust off of the bread.
4. Cut the sandwiches in triangles.

If you fill each sandwich with 1/3 level cup, you will get 10 sandwiches: 40 triangles.

If you fill each sandwich with ¼ level cup, you will get 14 sandwiches: 56 triangles.

These triangles are placed on top of paper doilies, which are set in an attractive tray, not on a plate. A tray is required so that the treasured sandwiches don't slide around.

At my new and beloved church, Keller UMC, I hosted a Christmas dinner for the Stephen Ministers. I decided to follow the New Fountain UMC tradition of pimento cheese sandwiches but with a little extra ingredient: horseradish. As I offered them to guests, I said, "Would you like a Sassy Pimento Cheese Sandwich?"

One guest, Bob, retracted his hand as he was about to grab a sandwich and exclaimed, "Oh, I want the non-sassy version."

Pastor Tom Faile, standing nearby, offered his opinion, "Bob, if you want non-sassy, you came to the wrong house." Pastor Tom was our minister when Mike and I got married, so he's pretty special to us. He did forget to say, "You may kiss your bride," and Mike protested, grabbing my arm as I turned to leave the altar. It was a pretty good kiss. It was the most fun moment of our wedding! We still laugh about it. We being Mike and me. Pastor Tom, not so much. We like to celebrate our anniversary with Pastor Tom and his wife, Pastor Meg Witmer-Faile, whom we call the Pastor of Radical Hospitality.

Not only are Pimento Cheese Sandwiches held to a standard, there is a strict expectation for Apricot Bar Cookies to appear at New Fountain UMC. There was a variation from each person who made them, (one person uses only almond extract, another uses only vanilla extract, and one person uses both) but they better be buttery. There's enough butter in them to make Paula Deen flash her beautiful smile and say, "There's butter in them, y'all." I don't know if she makes Apricot Bar Cookies, but if she did, they would be similar to this recipe. They are not a hard crunchy cookie, but a soft, melting moment kind of a cookie bar.

Apricot Bar Cookies

Preheat the oven to 350°. Prepare a 9" X 11" by greasing it or spraying with nonstick spray.

12 tablespoons (1 1/2 sticks) butter, room temperature

1 cup sugar

1 egg, room temperature

1/2 teaspoon vanilla extract

1/2 teaspoon almond extract

2 cups flour

1/4 teaspoon baking powder

1 cup shredded coconut

1 (18 ounce) jar apricot preserves

1. Cream butter and sugar until blended; add the egg, vanilla and almond extracts.
2. In a separate bowl, stir/whisk the flour and baking powder.
3. Gradually add this mixture to the butter mixture.
4. Add the coconut and stir until well-blended.
5. Put about 2/3 of the mixture in the prepared pan, pressing it to the edges.
6. Spread the apricot preserves over the crust.
7. Spread the remaining crust in small crumbles over the apricot.

Bake at 350° for 30 minutes and let cool in the pan on a wire rack. Cut into 18-24 bars and make sure you hide some before your family sees them or you won't get any.

At Keller UMC, when we have a gathering, I take Pimento Cheese Sandwiches in triangle shapes. It's the only time I buy white bread. One time, I made some on white bread and some on whole grain bread. I placed them in a symmetrically pleasing pattern, alternating white, wheat, white, wheat. I had only six triangles left—all wheat!

Keller UMC has some of the most loving and generous people who will provide comforting and soothing meals. I was a recipient of this love.

My parents died within twenty-four hours of each other Thanksgiving weekend, 2019. They were ninety-seven and ninety-six years old. They did not suffer. They didn't have a heart attack or a stroke or any disease. They just stopped living.

My mother died on Friday afternoon in their apartment with their caregiver by her side. My dad was hospitalized for very mild bronchitis and a low heart rate, which at age ninety-seven, was cause for concern. He was irate I wouldn't take him home. But he was so weak that he couldn't stand up. I tried to explain that at six foot five, he was too tall for me to catch. I reminded him that I, too, am considered elderly. I personally do not think that I am old. I am mature and experienced.

"Fine," he grumbled, "I'll just call an Uber."

"You can't call an Uber. You have to have an app," I explained.

"App! App! I don't even have a smartphone! I wanted you to get me a smartphone. How can I get home?" Ninety-seven years old and he's dismayed that he doesn't have a smartphone.

Dad kept insisting that he needed to get home to "take care of Betty." During this time, my parents' devoted caregiver was texting me that my mother was fading fast—not suffering, just fading from life.

My mother had been in hospice care for a tracheal obstruction, so when she transitioned, the hospice team went into action, appearing at the hospital to assess my dad. The hospice nurse, in conjunction with the hospital staff, decided to admit my dad into hospice care as his heart rate was dropping and he was so agitated.

My brothers were with our mother, taking care of calling the funeral home, relatives and other necessary calls, while I was at the hospital with Dad.

I asked to speak to the hospice doctor out in the hall. We were both wearing cheap, plastic holiday bulb necklaces—the kind that flash off and on. We thought that was a funny coincidence and it lightened, no pun intended, the somber moment.

I spoke softly, "You know my mom died a couple of hours ago?"

The doctor nodded and asked, "Yes, I know. How long were they married?"

"Almost seventy-eight years," I proclaimed with a small amount of pride, but also some amazement.

"That's why we have admitted your dad into our care. He'll need all of us. When will you tell him?" He looked like he might cry.

"When I can get him calmed down and get him some dinner. Is my dad dying?"

The doctor didn't hesitate, "Probably. His heart rate is dropping and when you tell him about your mother, he'll take it pretty hard."

I choked it out, "He's dying from what?"

The doctor cleared his throat and gently said, "I know you are a believer. I heard you praying with, and for, your dad. I want you to think about this. You and I only know earthly things, but at some level, he knows she's gone. I think he's dying of a broken heart. I know you haven't told him about your mother, but he knows. That's why he's so upset."

The doctor may have hummed as he quoted words to an old hymn,

Farther along, we'll know all about it. Farther along, we'll understand why.

My sister-in law, Sandra, arrived to keep me company and to help me with Dad. I ordered what would be his last meal. The man loved to eat! He especially loved to eat cookies. The hospital kitchen wouldn't let me order him a cookie.

"Why?" I demanded.

The poor clerk on the other end of the phone line was just doing her job and said, "Because he's on a heart healthy diet."

There momentarily was complete silence on my part. Disbelief. I was taken aback.

I wanted to scream, cry, demand. Instead, I politely pushed back, "He's ninety-seven years old. His wife of seventy-eight years just died, and I have to tell him. He needs a cookie."

Remember how Cookie Monster on Sesame Street said "cookie"? In a deep growly voice, speaking as if each letter is a syllable, C O O K I E. I think I may have growled it that same way, "He needs a C O O K I E!"

Luckily, Sandra had more wits about her than I did, and stepped in to order guest dinners for each of us; each dinner came with two cookies. And I'll bet you can guess who got those cookies.

Finally, he had eaten, knew he couldn't go home yet, and he settled down. He asked if he could call her. That opened the door for me to tell him.

"Dad, I 'm so sorry. Mom died this afternoon. She didn't hurt, she didn't suffer. She just finished living."

"Oh no!" he lamented, "I didn't get to tell her good-bye and kiss her good-bye."

"Well," I offered, "You've been faithful in kissing her hello and good-bye for almost seventy-eight years of marriage. I think she knew you loved her."

"Oh, well," he volunteered, "I kissed her before we got married."

"Alrighty then, that's a little TMI (too much information), but I'm glad you have happy memories." I quickly changed the subject.

I really didn't dread the next part of our conversation, which needed to be about what kind of service to have for my mother. More than fifteen years ago, my brothers and I had broached the topic of end-of-life decisions with our parents. We were just being proactive. We knew they would be around a long time. I still have those notes. Remember, I am The Notetaker.

"Dad, let's talk about the service for Mom. Years ago, she said she didn't want multiple services. What do you think?"

Dad did not hesitate, but what he said stopped my breathing. "Let's keep it low-key and just have a curbside service." Here I was for the second time in one evening being taken aback and momentarily completely silent.

Finally, I found my voice and asked, "Well, Dad, is a curbside service where people drive up to a window and wave good-bye? Or do they park at a curb and wave from there?" I guess my shock took over my sense of sobriety in the moment, and I just had to have some fun. My dad was not amused.

"NO!" he almost shouted, "You put up a tent and set out chairs."

"Ah, I get it. A graveside service," I offered affably, knowing that now was not the time to have any more fun.

"Yes, a graveside service, and I want Pastor Jim to conduct it. Can you call him and arrange that?"

I contacted Pastor Jim Chandler, who looks and sounds like the late Reverend Billy Graham, and has a voice that oozes comfort, like honey dripping off of a hot biscuit.

He's famous at our church for saying, "I feel a prayer coming on." Even though we've heard it many, many times, we still laugh when he says it. I repeated the curbside service story to Pastor Jim, and we had a good laugh, interspersed with crying and a few hiccupping moments.

After a moment of silence, my Dad lamented, "I was supposed to take care of her," and he drifted off to sleep. It made me sad to hear his disappointment in himself. Steadily through the night, his heart rate dropped.

The next morning, his long fingers were so cold and still, his heart rate continuing to drop and he had no awareness of any of us in the room. Kids and grandkids all gathered and told favorite stories about the man we called Grants. My mother had claimed the grandparent titles of Grammy and Gramps. Of course, as in many families, the first grandchild pronounces the names incorrectly, and everyone thinks it's so cute that the mispronounced names are adopted. So, my parents became Mammy and Grants instead of Grammy and Gramps. That's why we have such fun grandparents' names that are loosely based on what they wanted: PaPaw, Pappy, Pop Pop, Bapoo, Big Daddy, Big Mama, Omie, GiGi, Tutu, Gran Ma'am, Omaha, Britches, GoGo, Bubba, Poppy, and other terms of endearment.

I kept holding Dad's hands, wrapping them with warm towels and blankets. I don't know if it comforted him, but it comforted me. And then, twenty-four hours and ten minutes after I told him that mom had passed, he just stopped living. As stunned as we all were, I knew it was a bittersweet blessing that they went together.

The Nicholsons came to do whatever, stay with us, answer the door, put out food, the things that life-long friends and kitchen buddies do for each other. A few days later, we had a double curbside service. It literally was next to a curb, and Pastor Jim told the story of my dad asking for a curbside service and commented, "James, you got your curbside service." There was a flag ceremony, a Masonic service and grandchildren told sweet stories. My granddaughter, Addie, sang *Amazing Grace*, acapella, and made it to the last three words without crying.

I knew the Methodists would start appearing at our door. I just know them and their hearts that love and nurture others. If I tried to list them all, I might miss someone and hurt a beloved friend's feelings.

Our Sunday School class, The Pathfinders, showed up immediately, and other church members weren't too far behind. The Pathfinders had been listening for a very long time about my parents, especially when we took the car keys from my dad. That could be an entire chapter, but I'll spare you the bitter details. Suffice to say I am forever indebted to this extraordinary, smart, funny, and kind group of people. I should also describe them as generous. That, too, could be an entire chapter of the ways The Pathfinders serve other people. They participate in mission trips to distribute eyeglasses in Belize and water filters in a village in Haiti; adopting a family to provide a Thanksgiving meal, providing that same family with a Christmas meal and gifts for all family members; organize an annual golf tournament to benefit our Resource Center; volunteer at the Resource Center; participate in church leadership service as ushers, communion servers, marathon pandemic mask-makers and more. When one of us has a need, we gather on the doorstep, on the phone, on an email trying to help in any way. Emmanuel in action.

There are so many groups at our church that serve so many. The Sisters of Sewing were like a car that can go from zero to sixty in a couple of seconds when the pandemic began. Seriously, they flew into action, making thousands of masks, trading fabric, sharing the hard-to-find elastic, leaving finished products on someone's porch who would deliver it to a hospital, doctors' office, a senior residential center or any family that needed masks. Emmanuel in action.

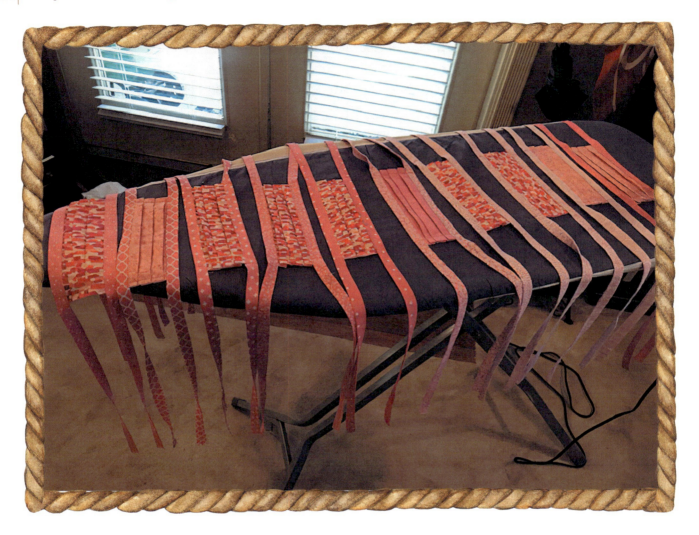

My mom died on Friday, my dad died on Saturday, and The Methodists, several Baptists, and an Atheist arrived at our door on Sunday and for many days afterward with:

- Pimento Cheese Sandwiches cut in triangles—you knew that was coming!
- a pepper plant and a bag of chocolate,

- an orchid,
- gallon jug of tea,
- gallon jug of vodka with a bag of limes and a bag of ice,
- Chicken Spaghetti,
- Taco Soup, chips, salad and sweet jalapeno jelly to pour over a block of cream cheese,
- a variety of sandwiches, and salads from a local sandwich shop, with two kinds of wine to help all that food go down easily,
- Pot Roast with potatoes and carrots,
- Spaghetti, salad and garlic bread,
- another gallon jug of vodka with two bags of limes,
- certificates for food delivery,
- gift cards to local restaurants,
- Bourbon Pecan Pie,
- King Ranch Chicken and Hawaiian Rolls,
- deli meats and cheese platter,
- sausage and sauerkraut, with hot mustard and pretzel rolls,
- grilled hamburgers, baked French fries,
- a Rose of Sharon/Althea plant to plant in our yard,
- Cranberry Pecan Bars,
- and so much more!

Scripture Cake

	Ch.	Verse		
1 Kings	4	22	3½ cups	flour
Judges	5	25	1 cup	milk
Judges	4	19	1 cup	
Jeremiah	6	20	2 cups	
Nahum	3	12	2 cups	
I Samuel	30	12	2 cups	
I Samuel	14	25	2 Tbs.	
Amos	4	5	3½ teaspoon	
Jeremiah	17	11	Use 4	
Leviticus	2	13	¼ Teaspoon	
II Chronicles	9	9	1 Teaspoon each	

After finding the ingredients in the scripture follow these directions: Cream butter & sugar. Add beaten eggs yolks, honey, milk & 3 cups flour which has been sifted with the spices & baking powder. Use the remaining ½ cup flour for the fruit. Add beaten egg whites before fruit & flour are added. Bake in greased floured pans. at 350° for 60 min.

Scripture Cake

A sweet note to close this chapter is the Scripture Cake from my aunt's recipe book, in her handwriting, a very old recipe called the **Scripture Cake.**

Please note that the ingredients in the text version of the **Scripture Cake** appear in a **different** order than in the photo of the handwritten version. In the text, the ingredients are listed in order they will be used in the recipe. The handwritten recipe was recorded by my aunt in the 1940s in a Sunday School class. The handwritten version is inexact for baking, but it is charming in its spiritual references. The legend of the Scripture Cake is that was a way to teach cooking and the Bible at the same time. I had one of my editors taste-test this cake. She described it as being like "Mother's Day, Thanksgiving, and Christmas Day all rolled into one." I think the Pinot Noir helped, but it is a tasty cake!

Preheat the oven to 350°. Grease and flour or spray with nonstick baking spray six (2 1/2" X 4 1/2") mini loaf pans and one regular (8" X 4") loaf pan **OR** two regular (8" X 4") loaf pans.

1 cup butter (Judges 5:25)
2 cups sugar (Jeremiah 6:20)
4 eggs separated (Jeremiah 17:11)
2 tablespoons honey (I Samuel 14:25)
1 cup milk (Judges 4:19)
3 1/4 cups flour, will be divided (I Kings 4:22)
1/2 teaspoon cinnamon (II Chronicles 9:9)
1/4 teaspoon nutmeg
1/4 teaspoon allspice
1/2 teaspoon salt
3 1/2 teaspoons of baking powder
2 cups raisins (I Samuel 30:12)
1 cup slivered almonds

1. Cream butter and sugar.
2. Separate the white and the yolks of the eggs
3. Whisk the yolks. Set the whites aside.
4. Add the egg yolks, honey, milk to the butter mixture.
5. Sift 3 cups of the flour with the cinnamon, nutmeg, allspice, salt and baking powder.
6. Add the flour mixture to the butter mixture.
7. Whisk the egg whites until frothy.
8. Add the egg whites to the butter & flour mixture.
9. Add the remaining 1/2 cup flour, the almonds and the raisins. Fold this into the mixture.

Bake at 350° for 60 minutes.

TIPS & HINTS

- If you don't have a Food Saver System© , request one for the next occasion or just go buy one. There may be other systems like this, but I don't know about them. I use ours every week. I check the Manager's Special bin in the meat department, and if there are two or more items, I buy them and freeze them when I get home. When chicken thighs go on sale, I buy ten to twenty pounds and divide the packages into three or four thighs. Here's an important tip, which I learned the hard way. I know, I should have read the directions. I am saving you a headache and a big mess here. You must slightly pre-freeze the food before you put it through the *shrink-wrap* process, otherwise, the juice runs into the suction tray. That's a big mess! When The Methodists, The Baptists, and The Atheist arrived, they brought enough food for several people, some of it soup. To freeze soup, get a muffin tin that makes huge muffins, spray it with a non-stick spray, ladle the soup in, and let it freeze until it's not juicy. After you put it through the process, it will last for more than a year. It may last longer than that, but I haven't tested anything beyond a year and a couple of months. I so hate wasting food, or anything for that matter, and this method means no more freezer burn.

- I've read and tried many, many options for Pimento Cheese. I personally like to add a tablespoon of horseradish, unless I'm serving it to kids. Kids don't usually like horseradish. Here are other additives I've read about, and have tried a few:

  - 1/2 cup of stout beer
  - 1/4 cup of chopped nuts – I've used walnuts and loved that addition!
  - 1/4 cup grated onions
  - 1 tsp of garlic powder
  - chopped parsley
  - cayenne pepper
  - 1/4 cup chopped green olives
  - a splash of Worcestershire sauce
  - a splash or more of Tabasco sauce

- If you take food to someone's home, enclose an index card with the foods you provided. That way, they don't have to guess what they are eating, and they don't have to rely on their memory when they want to thank you.

- If you are the lucky recipient of a meal or some goodies, have a running list of who brings what. You won't remember after about three or four people!

Now it's time to thank you for:

- Hopping on your horse and joining me for a ride,

- Nodding your head and saying yes to planning your next great meal!

- Step off and being so prepared that you are ready to relax and enjoy your guests, and

- Focus, focus, focus on what you've achieved, what memories you have created and how much love you have expressed for others.

Conclusion

Don't Swing Too Fast, Don't Swing Too Slow: How to Keep Improving as a Cook

I could dance with you until the cows come home. On second thought, I'd rather dance with the cows until you come home.

Groucho Marx

Terry and Jody wave goodbye!

Many ropers have friends or family video them as they enter the box, nod their head, rope, step off, and tie down. A video in the SloMo mode helps a roper see they built a loop too big, if they swing too fast, if they swing too slow or any number of other mistakes.

In addition to a video, ropers practice with each other and offer advice such as:

- Settle your horse in the box
- Focus
- Make your loop smaller
- Keep elbows up
- Pitch rope slack quickly
- Lean forward in your saddle

Paying attention to getting better at anything and everything is part of success. The same is true of planning, prepping, and serving meals. A video of prepping a meal is impractical as it would be way too long.

Feedback and continuous learning is vital to getting better as a cook (and as a human)! The feedback may be overt, "This is too salty," or covert, as in, they leave most of a serving on their plate. Feedback from yourself can be helpful as you cook. The instructor in one of the cooking classes reminded us that we must taste our food multiple times during the cooking and use a clean tasting spoon each time.

When you serve a meal, you can notice for yourself if the dish needs more salt, less garlic or a boost in heat. In Texas, adding heat is a part of many meals, but as I said before, I like for my guests and meal recipients to add their own peppers. If it is just for Mike and me, I'll ramp it up, and I usually double any measurements for garlic.

Feedback is great but has some limitations. Everyone's taste is different, and your friends and family might not be completely candid! They love you and want to support you! That's a good thing!

The value of your feedback to yourself is limited as well, because self-reporting is dependent on you having great self-awareness and noticing what *needs* to be addressed rather than what you prefer to notice.

I often give myself feedback by writing on a recipe, specifically about timing. For example, I have a recipe for sea scallops with lots of Italian seasonings, kale, and any kind of white canned beans. After the first time I made it, I wrote:

> *This moves fast! Have everything chopped and lined up and don't let anyone talk to you while you're cooking.*

What are ways to get better as a cook? Here are my favorites:

Volunteer for Vacation Bible School or whatever your community of faith offers to kids and teens!

Yes, VBS! You will be with women and men who have a heart to serve others and the conversation always turns to "*What's for dinner?*" If you are in my age group, you'll hear new recipes, about new appliances, and herbs and spices you haven't used. Hang out with the younger, or older, generation and learn what you can from them. And don't make excuses about being too old, already having volunteered when your kids were little, etc. Stretch yourself and help out!

Take Cooking Classes

My two favorites are my Cook and Write Retreats and classes at kitchen stores. Cook and Write retreats are a favorite because of the reflection, the writing, and the examination of memories of food. We are sharing more than recipes. We're sharing life, love, memories, and ways to reframe and approach challenges. In the picture, you see the facilitators, Lyn and Beverly, preparing to serve a meal that our participants cooked.

And, of course, the food looks so inviting, and tastes so mouthwatering that participants just pause and appreciate before diving in.

We linger at the table and hear the group who cooked share their memories of the recipe they made.

Cooking classes at a store that sells kitchen equipment has several positive points and one tiny heads-up. The recipes are vetted so you know they've been tested and will be dangerously delicious. The ingredients are already chopped up—who wouldn't LOVE that to be the case at home?!

The ingredients are not only already chopped up, they are measured for you, and lined up as you add them to the recipe. I generally do this at home, but I'd be just fine with a Kitchen Fairy flitting in to do it for me!

Another thing I like about cooking classes at a kitchen store is that the same little kitchen fairy dashes in to clean up!

A benefit and a tiny heads-up are that the chef works for the store, and they sell beautiful dishes, tools, tea towels, and high-quality cookware in sets that cost more than my first car. (It wasn't much of a car). During cooking classes, they will offer a discount if you buy it while at the store. So, decide before you go what you might want to buy and set a budget. There will always be a sale on something. Wait for it! But keep in mind that if you need or want something, they offer pretty nice discounts.

Wander Around the Internet and See What Bloggers have to say

I recently found *Ten Tips to Immediately Improve Your Cooking* on sharedappetitie.com. The blogger, Chris, actually offers *eleven* and not just *ten tips.* He offered a bonus tip! My favorites include:

- *Get Out of the Recipe Straight Jacket.* He reminds us that no recipe is perfect for every person in every kitchen. He encourages us to trust our instincts, watch and experience your food as it cooks. Use the recipe as a guideline, not an absolute rule.

- *Think Texture.* Chris says that a plain turkey sandwich is boring. Add a creamy dressing, a ripe tomato, and some crunchy lettuce.

I recently tore a recipe out of a magazine for Butternut Squash Noodles with Spinach. I thought it needed more crunch, so I sprinkled toasted pine nuts on top. Then I thought, "Hey, if spinach works, I'll bet a handful of kale will work, too!" I used both and just made it more interesting!

- *Eat with Your Eyes*. Chris says that we eat with our eyes first, and presentation matters. He suggests that if you are serving a red soup, add a green garnish. If you're serving green steamed veggies, add a dollop of plain yogurt or sour cream, or a newly discovered, freshly grated cheese.

Watch Cooking Shows and Cooking Segments from News and Talk Shows

I watch a few cooking shows that I love and some I don't really love. But I always learn something. In cooking and in my personal, professional, and political life, I like to interact with ideologies and techniques with which I have some discomfort. It forces me to grow and to remember that usually we have more in common than we have in differences. Therefore, watching cooking shows that make me uncomfortable also make me think differently.

Tips and Hints

(I *want* to follow but have to make myself follow)

- Take meat out of the refrigerator and let it get closer to room temperature before cooking.

- When measuring sugar, just scoop it out of your container with your measuring cup; when it's flour, spoon it into your measuring cup and level it off with a straight edge. I did notice on two recent cooking shows that some notable chefs just scoop flour out!

- When meat is finished with the cooking cycle, let it rest. I am always ready to cut into it, especially steak, ribs, roast . . . okay, any meat. However, we need to let meat rest so that the juices can redistribute and the meat can continue to cook a bit. Leave it alone! Set a Timer! Five minutes!

- Use different chopping boards for different foods:
  - One for uncooked meat, chicken seafood
  - One for cooked meats
  - One for vegetables, fruits, bread

Thanks for riding on this journey with me. Friends, my prayer, my hope and my wish for you is that you

Cowboys' Prayer

By Baxter Black

Dear Lord,

Yer lookin' at a man who never learned to cook,
unless you count pork and beans.
And a flowery grace like you'd read in a book,
is really beyond my means.

But you can believe I'm a thankful man
though it might be undeserved.
And I'll eat whatever comes out of the pan,
no matter what's bein' served.

I don't take it lightly if it's real good,
'cause I'd eat it anyway.
See I know there's people, in all likelihood,
that might not eat today.

So count me in if yer needin' grace said,
and bless those who provide it.
The farmers and ranchers, the bakers of bread,
the loving hands that fried it.

But most of all, Lord, we give thanks to You,
'cause we who work on the land,
Know how much our harvest and bounty is due
to the gainful touch of Yer hand.

So bless this food and the life we embrace,
And please forgive us our pride.
When others with tables a-plenty say grace,
for what we've helped You provide.

Reprinted with Author Permission from his column "On the Edge of Common Sense." 1984.

Acknowledgements

- Mike – you hold my heart in your hands.

- Paul and Gracie – you inspired me, and still inspire me, to be a better person and I love you dearly.

- Eric and Juli – you make my children so happy and your children are the cutest and smartest in the whole world.

- Hunter and Addie Westbrook; Mason, Camden and Libby Packwood – I've probably bought over one hundred books for you, but this one I partially wrote for you. Always remember our Cousins' Camps!

- All ten of the Bergman grandchildren – I look forward to more opportunities to cook with you!

- Cook & Write leaders, Beverly Charles and Lyn Mefford and fellow participants – I stand on your shoulders.

- Beverly Charles – my writing coach, friend, fellow Star Learner, spiritual friend and the best lipstick wearer ever!

- Dr. Lyn Mefford – you have shared so much with so many; you give unconditional love, you share your space, your wit, your time, your intellect and your heart.

- Nicholsons – Karen, Jim, Jamie Lankes and Jody Bell – for many years of food and fun, learning and asking, laughing and hanging pictures in every empty space we can find.

- Terry Morganti-Fisher – my Sister of Choice, a fellow Star Leaner, who supports and challenges me, makes me laugh, lets me cry.

- Pete Mefford – Sweet Pete! A writer who is generous with thoughts, time, and wine.

- Dr. Linda O'Neal – a fellow Star Learner, a model of how to repurpose anything and everything – furniture, a friendship, a life, and how to wonder instead of fret.

- The late Dr. Shirley Hord – I was not succinct or crisp in my writing, but you would have loved the stories!

- The Late Janet Bliss Mello – friend, fellow Star Learner, mentor, mentee, now a Blingy Star in Heaven.

- New Fountain United Methodist Church – you matured my spiritual life and showed me how to do more than believe; you showed me how to follow.

- Keller UMC Pathfinders Sunday School – How lucky we are to be a class; we learn together; we laugh together; we play together, we help others together and we worship together. If any of you have to take the car away from an elderly parent, you all know that I'm the expert in this gruesome task. Call me, you have earned my attention by listening to many years of stories.

- Diane and Tommy – part of the roper family and technical advisors.

- Fabulous chefs from whom I learn – the list grows all the time.

- Marilyn Gondolf and Susan Yarborough – for your 24/7 loving and patient care of my parents for three and a half tough years. On the Monday shift change, when I delivered that night's dinner, you were always gracious and grateful.

- Dr. Peter Kahle – for moving me past my fear. Your wit, spirituality and intellect provided great guidance and compassionate questions.

- My brothers, Jim Mason and Porter Mason – for three kids who weren't taught to cook, we somehow figured it out and even got pretty good at it!

- My mother, the late Betty Foote Mason – you expected the best from me in all that I did.

- And finally, my dad, the late James Leon Mason. Your thirty years of writing the newsletter for the Southwestern Bell Telephone Credit Union, then thirty years of writing the newsletter for the retired telephone company workers made me think writing is just something we do. And then, of course, there was the writing of letters to the traffic department, to the mayor and the city council, and to anyone who said they were an atheist. Additionally, your stage presence as you served as Master of Ceremonies for a variety of gatherings made me think that talking to hundreds of adults is like talking to a friend, and I followed your lead and taught large groups for many years. Your willingness to teach Defensive Driving until you were ninety years old was a model of tenacity. As Toby Keith sings it, *Don't Let the Old Man In,* and you never did. Rest in Peace.

References & Resources

Beck, K. and Clark, J. (1995). *The All-American Cowboy Cookbook.*
    Nashville: Rutledge Hill Press, p. 33.

Bell, L. P. (1932). *Kitchen Fun: A Cook Book for Children*.
    Cleveland: The Harter Publishing Company, p. 1.

Black, B. "*On the Edge of Common Sense",* 1994.
    www.baxterblack.com

Chavez, C. https://www.goodreads.com/quote

Childs, J. https://www.atlanta.eats.com/blog/aologize-lesson-juliachilds

Cockren, C., (2021). *Ten Tips to Immediately Improve Your Cooking*. [online]
    Shared Appetite. Available at: <https://sharedappetite.com>

Conroy, P. (2004). *The Pat Conroy Cookbook.* New York: Doubleday, p. 20.

Craven, M. (1967). *I Heard the Owl Call My Name.* Toronto:
    Clarke, Irwin & Company, p. 77.

Crocker, B. (1957). *Betty Crocker's Cook Book for Boys and Girls.* New York:
    Simon and Schuster, p. 186.

Crocker, B. (1967). *Hostess Cookbook.* 1 ed. New York: Golden Press, p. 9.

Fieri, G. https://www.brainyquote.com/topics.

Forrest Gump. 1994. [DVD]. Savannah GA. The Tisch Company.

Garten, I. (2014). *Make It Ahead.* New York: Clarkson Potter, pp. 11-12.

Goodwin, M. (2020). '7 Tips for Teaching Children to Cook', Frugal and Thriving,
        30 December. https://frugalandthriving.com.

Hannon, A. N. (2017). *love, welcome, serve.* New York: Center Street, p.X.

Hauk, H. "Ree Drummond." *Cowboys and Indians*, Volume 28, Number 1, January, 2020.

Holy Bible, New International Version→, NIV→. Copyright 1973,1978,1984,2011 by Biblica, Inc.

Holy Bible, King James Version. 1976. New York: Regency Publishing House.

https://www.ifunny.com/memes.

Johnson, B. and Randolph, R. (2013). *We Laugh, We Cry, We Cook.* Grand Rapids:
        Zondervan, p. 4.

Kartes, D. (2020). *Meant to Share.* Naperville: Sourcebooks, p. xvii.

Lonesome Dove. 1985. [DVD]. Del Rio TX. Motown Production.

Marx, G. https://www.quotationspage.com/subjects.

Metcalfe, G. and Hays, C. (2005). *Being Dead is No Excuse.* New York: Miramax, p. 83.

People. 2018. Ian Garten, The Ultimate Hostess. (Special Edition), p. 26.

Ray, R. (2005). *30-Minute Get Real Meals.* New York: Clarkson Potter, p. X

Rachael Ray Show. 2017. *Recipes.* [online] Available at:
        <https://www.rachaelrayshow.com/recipes>.

Spears, G. and Brigit B. (2000). *Cowboy Cocktail.* Berkeley: Ten Speed Press, p.9.

Sroufe, D. 2019. Cooking at Every Age, Why Kids Should learn to Cook. [Blog]
        [online] https://nutritionstudies.org

Stewart, M. (2009). *Dinner at Home.* New York: Clarkson Potter.

Woerner, G. H. (2007). *Rope to Win.* Fort Worth: Eakin Press, p. 10.

Recipe Index

A portion of the author's proceeds go to these missions, and other missions as needed:

- The Keller UMC Resource Center, which provides food, paper goods, diapers and cleaning supplies to families in our community.

More information about this mission is available at:

Keller United Methodist Church
Cathy Dill, Director of Serving Ministries
1025 Johnson Road
Keller, Texas 76248
817. 431.1332
cathyd@kellerumc.org
www.kellerumc.org

- Water to Life, whose mission is to provide access to clean water and educational opportunities to people and areas that lack these vital resources.

More information about this mission is available at:

Keith Bierley, Secretary/Treasurer
1025 Johnson Road
Keller, Texas. 76248
817.657.9697
keithbierley@charter.net
www.watertolife.org

Printed in the United States
By Bookmasters